The
I Do's & I Don'ts
of a Successful Marriage

The
I Do's & I Don'ts
of a Successful Marriage

Rick L. Cox

authorHOUSE®

AuthorHouse™ LLC
1663 Liberty Drive
Bloomington, IN 47403
www.authorhouse.com
Phone: 1-800-839-8640

Published by AuthorHouse   10/26/2013

ISBN: 978-1-4685-4262-2 (sc)
ISBN: 978-1-4685-4261-5 (hc)
ISBN: 978-1-4685-4260-8 (e)

Library of Congress Control Number: 2013919594

TABLE OF CONTENTS

To Judy, who is and always has been the love of my life. She has very much helped to even out the lows and highs of my life.

To my two lovely daughters, Riki and Lindsay, who have helped me to learn immensely about life and how it works.

Many thanks to all three of you for being the best part of me.

Special thanks also to Mr. Leonard Keene, who long ago completed his journey here on earth. He had an incredible impact on my personal and married life through his Balanced Life Seminar teaching.

Finally, I am grateful to the editing staff at AuthorHouse for their enduring patience with me, as well as their valuable help with the completion and form of this book. Their comments helped me to grow, as well as expand my thinking. More importantly, they made it look as if I knew how to write.

FOREWORD

To say the institution of marriage is under assault today is an understatement that any keen observer of culture will not take long to conclude. What has been not only ordained by God but accepted by all peoples and religions as the accepted institutional model has been bombarded with attacks from the inherent selfishness of mankind. No wonder about half of all marriages end up in divorce, and the statistic is far from getting better. One can just imagine the long-term effects of this tragedy on the succeeding generations. Not to mention how many couples allow themselves to be cheated from experiencing the joy of true marital bliss, as well as the potential growth and maturity such a union can provide to each individual.

But there is much hope! For one thing, the grand designer of marriage has laid out a very clear blueprint that can help couples not only survive the assaults on their relationship but actually thrive and bring it to the highest level in fulfilling the purposes originally intended for them. Along with this blueprint there are those who have been raised up to help us better comprehend these guidelines through the writing of their own experiences. Their hope is to help us choose a correct path by following a better way.

Leadership expert John Maxwell wrote, "We can teach people what we know, but we can only reproduce who we are." Rick Cox does not only teach in this book what he knows, but more importantly he seeks to reproduce himself both through his many years of coming alongside hurting couples and honestly sharing of his own marriage journey. He does not offer any quick fix for marital troubles but, through his own life example, shares simple, practical, and down-to-earth daily marriage-building habits that have helped lay a strong and enduring foundation to over four decades of successful marriage to his lovely wife.

We can turn the tide of deteriorating relational values in our generation. And since the family is the so-called smallest battle formation in any society, married couples are the critical pacesetters called by God to be intimate allies of this force. As marriages succeed, we can change society, one home at a time, while moving toward and enjoying the blessings of a fruitful and fulfilling marriage.

I cannot more heartily recommend Rick Cox's work and invite you to join the marriage revolution, one marriage and one home at a time!

Dr. Arthur F. Guina
The Jesus Film Project
Campus Crusade for Christ, Int'l.

INTRODUCTION

**Marriage is the toughest of all relationships, taking an
immense effort from each party if it is to be successful
and long-lasting.**

As of this writing, I have been fortunate to be married to the same
lady for almost four decades. In that time, we have been through a
lot of trials and tribulations that have put a tremendous strain on our
relationship. I have found that commitment to working through the
tough and trying times is the key to maintaining a healthy and happy
relationship. Acting on your feelings will most often cause nothing but
trouble for the long-term success of your marriage.

This trouble is often the consequence of unschooled emotions. When
unschooled emotions run wild, the results are often the yelling of harsh
words, throwing objects at each other or at the wall, or even physical
violence toward one another. These actions cannot be taken back, nor will
they be forgotten.

Oddly enough, the premarital relationship starts out with the funny
butterflies and overwhelming emotions, as you are totally infatuated.
Then, depending on how quickly one moves ahead into this relationship,
the infatuation begins to decrease. As the infatuation decreases, you begin
to see faults to which you were previously blinded. As these faults become
more evident, you begin to second-guess your choice. You may begin to
treat the person with whom you were once so in love with disdain and
disrespect, causing the relationship to crumble.

Unfortunately, some never try to figure out what is wrong and wind
up staying in these damaged relationships, which adversely affects not
only their own life but also the lives of all those around them. Rather
than try to fix what is wrong or come to an understanding of why it went

wrong, they go underground, feigning to be people they are not in order to keep peace in the home and in the relationship. Thus, the majority of the homes and relationships today are producing children who do not understand commitment and are used to seeing people play what appears to be a game of charades. As a result, our offspring embark on their journey of doing the same. And so the majority of us wind up the by-product of how a marriage should not be rather than what it should be.

I was raised in one of these homes, but I was fortunate enough to get through the same games you just read about. By getting through these tough and trying times, I learned a few things that I believe can change your life and relationships for the better.

So, I share with you what I have learned from hands-on experience and not so much through that which can be found in books or classes or seminars. It isn't that you cannot learn via the aforementioned methodologies, for you can. What I have seen more often than not, however, is that the author or teacher or seminar instructor is often simply good at writing, teaching, or speaking. I have found that they can take what others have written and articulate it through their ability to craft a sentence and emotionalize their tone during a speech—and voilà, they gain an audience. Unfortunately in many cases, these individuals have no relevant personal experience.

I can still vividly remember when my wife and I attended a class on marriage and proper child rearing. The teacher had a PhD on the subject of relational psychology, as well as child behavior and parenting. There were approximately 150 people, or 75 couples, in that class, all of whom had at least one child or, in many cases, several children under the age of ten. From the very first class, many of us (me especially) did not feel this young man had any relevant personal experience in that which he was teaching. We did not feel he had ever actually applied what he was telling us do to. Although he was a good speaker and was able to emotionalize and articulate, there was something missing.

This was a twelve-week course lasting two hours per class. By the end of the first hour of the third class, I did not believe he was sharing something he knew worked. I was quite certain he had not actually tried what he was telling us to do, and thus I did not believe he knew it would work. He was simply stating what he had been taught by others, and he was assuming it would work.

There was a break between each hour, so at the start of the second hour I asked Dr. Smith (fictitious name) a couple questions. "Doctor, if you don't mind me asking, are you married? And if you are, how long have you been married? Secondly, do you have children? And if so, what are their ages?"

His answers to both stunned the majority of the class, but not me. He said, "I am not married, but I was and am now divorced. I have no children from that first marriage or any other relationship."

I then further asked him how he could be an expert on marriage and relationships if he was unable to make the first one work. I also asked if he believed the divorce taught him more about how to have a good marriage the second time around, and if so, if a third one would be better.

I continued by saying I had a friend that had been married three times in ten years who felt his odds of finding a "good one" were getting better due to the numbers game he was playing. To me the only game my friend was playing was finding a woman that would do what he wanted the way he wanted it, and then he would be happy. My friend's wife would not be a wife but a servant.

Next I asked how he could possibly know if what he was telling us to do with regard to child rearing actually worked if he had not applied it himself. At this point the rest of those in the class began asking their own questions, and this chaos continued until the end of our hour. As a result of our questions and doubts concerning his true knowledge and ability regarding the rearing of a child or how to have a good marriage, the teacher wound up canceling this class.

With that being said, I have done my best to put into simple words what I believe makes a marriage successful. What is written on the following pages has worked for me and my wife, as well as for hundreds of others. I am sure, if you properly apply these concepts, they will work for you as well.

CHAPTER 1

The Importance of Correct Spousal Interaction: Part 1

DURING A NEW YEAR's holiday, incorrect spousal interaction took place between my wife and me, which brought to mind the main reason some marriages work well and some do not. Before I get into that, however, let me say there are many factors behind a successful marriage, the least of which is both parties giving 110 percent, as well as both placing successful marriage at the top of the priority list. That being said, I believe the single most important factor in a successful marriage is how we respond or react to the actions or attitudes of each other.

> **"Without hard work a marriage will appear like two broken hearts, looking like houses, where nobody lives."**
> **—Roger Miller**

As is common in most marriages, one spouse can at times get on the nerves of the other or do something that may annoy the other. Such was the case during this particular holiday. Usually it's the little things that put me off or upset me. Once I make up my mind, I am not one given easily to change at the last moment. My wife, on the other hand, can roll with any punch and mold or change, as necessary. I only wish, in this aspect, I was as good as her. The upside is the two of us make a great match, as we are truly opposites, working well at keeping each other in balance. That is to say it works well when we correctly respond to each other.

During this holiday, I allowed something she did and said to put me in a horrible mood. In retrospect, it now seems childish that I allowed the spoken words and actions of my wife to alter and ruin my day. For me, it is usually those closest to me, whom I allow to do this, rather than coworkers or friends. In general, I believe it works the same way for the majority of us.

There are many contributing factors to a successful marriage, but the greatest factor is correct spousal interaction.

This is based on personal observations of the interactions of people around me. For instance, as a boy, if I acted up or was not doing what I was told, and my dad had to get involved, his frequent comment was "Well, I hope you are happy, son. You have ruined my day!" At the time, I carried the guilt of ruining my dad's day. As I grew older, I began to realize I didn't have the power to ruin his or anyone's day unless they allowed it. The same is true in my case; my wife does not have the power to ruin my life or my day unless I give it to her. The same is true in anyone's case. No one has the power over you that you do not give them.

What it all boiled down to was that she made plans with a few of our coupled friends, which in essence included me driving her and those friends around. As a nondrinker, I always wind up being the designated driver for those who drink. In this case I was very upset, because she made these plans and committed me to them, never asking if I would mind. She had committed me to driving around all night with a group of people I knew would be drunk and obnoxious in no time. She also knew I had made previous plans and preferred not to spend time driving a bunch of drunken people around, especially the ones in this group.

Previous to the start of her planned evening, I had nearly two hours to figure out how I was going to politely and correctly let her have a piece of my mind. By the end of the two hours, I had calmed down and had put together what I believed was the right thing to say. In my opinion, she needed to understand what she did and how it made me feel—as if she didn't know after thirty-seven years of marriage (at that time).

Of course, after all the years of marriage, she knew, but in my haste to get this off my chest and thereby make myself feel better, I chose a route. I am quite sure the love doctor would not have recommended the route I chose. What I wanted to do was make her feel the pain I felt, as well as make her feel bad about presupposing I would do something and committing me to it without first asking.

It is common to dump the guilt of a bad reaction on those closest to us in order to relieve ourselves of carrying it. This is also the main reason for broken marriages.

Now, if she had maliciously done something to belittle or hurt me, one might justify my methodology. I am not saying the direction she took was right; I simply said one might try to justify it. The direction or methodology I took is not that which my wife would have taken. Even if she had said or done something demeaning, the wise thing would not have been to allow her to control my life. This, nevertheless, is exactly what I would have been doing had I continued to be angry at her. When you are angry and bitter at someone, you are, in essence, giving control of your life to that person. You are allowing that person's words or actions— be they good, bad, or indifferent—to determine what you say, do, or become.

As a responsible adult, not being incarcerated and living in a free society, there should be no need to have someone monitoring and overseeing our lives, but that, in fact, is what can happen when we become angry and bitter at others. Through the anger and bitterness we are assigning this position to others by default. This keeps us tied to their influence and, in some cases, their control of our lives. It seems to me we are a bit too old to be giving others control of our lives, yet husbands and wives do this every single day by default when they get angry and bitter at each other, allowing this anger and bitterness to cause a break in their relationship. In this case I am fortunate, as my wife has never wanted control of me, nor has she tried to gain it. If more women took this same high road, I believe a substantial amount of marriages would still be working.

It just so happened, right after figuring out what I should have said, a large group of us were loading into my extended SUV. We were, as a group, headed to a few places that evening, with yours truly as the designated driver. Having a larger vehicle allowed everyone to enjoy themselves while driver boy took them wherever they wanted to go. As everyone was entering the vehicle, my wife loudly said, "Honey, you are always so understanding and so giving and would do anything for anybody. You are awesome. You are the best. I love you so much."

**"A soft answer turns away anger and will work toward
keeping as well as restoring relationships."
—Proverbs of Solomon**

To say she let the air out of my inflated tire of anger is an understatement. She didn't simply let the air out; she shot so many holes in it I forgot what the whole incident was about other than that she loved me and made me out to be the best thing in her life in front of everyone. At this point, I was king! I couldn't even tell you why I was angry, but I bet she knew (and might still know). The difference between me and her is she also knew what to do about it. She spoke words of encouragement, adulation, and praise. Most importantly, she spoke words of love.

The direction my wife took and the words she spoke constitute the correct spousal interaction. What she did was diffuse my anger with words of kindness. Proverbs says, "A soft answer turns away wrath." How true this is. Proverbs also says, "A word fitly spoken is like apples of gold in pictures of silver." Her soft words were definitely apples of gold and definitely diffused my anger. What a woman. By the way, this works in all aspects of life and in all relationships.

If both the husband and wife take direction from my wife, most marriages would be successful. Give it a try. I believe you will like the results.

CHAPTER 2

The Importance of Correct Spousal Interaction: Part 2

In chapter 1, some of you, especially the ladies, might have thought I cut the guys some slack by allowing them to have a less-than-favorable attitude, which could be covered by the loving wife, as long as she responded correctly to his undesirable behavior. On the other hand, a few of you guys might have thought I overlooked the fact that some women have similar behavior or worse and can be just as damaging. Ah, but this is far from the truth. I have not overlooked either one, for they will both be discussed in depth.

In the previous chapter, I used my own marriage as an example of what can happen when the husband gets bent out of shape. As you saw, the wife can, with the correct response, lessen and remove (or at the very least cause the husband to rethink) his selfish behavior. Just because I happen to be a guy and just because it is more often than not the guy who is to blame, this is not always the case. There are exceptions to every rule. But whether it is the husband or the wife, there are repercussions that affect the home, but we will deal with this in later chapters.

We all have good and bad days, with the exception perhaps of my wife. She goes to bed happy and wakes up happy. It may seem weird, but it has been this way since the first morning we woke up together, the morning after our wedding. Don't scoff or laugh—it really is true. Not only is the part about her being happy true, but the part about us waking up together for the first time after getting married is true, as well.

**All human beings have good and bad days or some days
that go better than others. It is your response to what
happens that determines a day that is bad or good.**

In most cases, the good and bad days are the result of our reactions to outside influences, which we allow to affect our behavior. How your life partner responds to your behavior will not only make a difference in the home atmosphere, but it can also make a difference in how long you remain in this funk. So our response to what our spouse says or does can play a major part in the overall outcome of the situation and in our life in general. A selfish, arrogant spouse will simply say what comes to mind first, without thinking. The end result of this open-mouth-and-insert-foot attitude is usually a heated argument. On the other hand, a wise spouse will know to respond properly to avoid a heated argument similar to the way my wife did in chapter 1.

Before we continue, it is important to make sure your marriage has the correct foundation. To have a strong foundation there has to be recognition that marriage is not a fifty-fifty partnership. In order for a marriage to be successful, both parties must give no less than 100 percent to the success of the marriage. This means it is not my wife's fault; it is my fault. It is not my husband's fault; it is my fault. When both parties give 100 percent to the marriage, it will work. This is the type of commitment it will take if the marriage is to make it in the long term.

**Marriages work best when both parties give 100 percent
without reservation for self.**

What I am saying is your wife isn't someone to pick on just to make yourself feel better. Your wife is not your guilt dump or the reason you are having a bad day. She is not why things aren't going well in your life, nor is she a pincushion into which you stick your pins of disappointment just so you can feel better. No, gentlemen, you need to learn to own up to, as well as deal with, your own issues.

You will find if you treat and respond to your wife correctly, she will more than likely be able to help you through many tough personal crises. As we all know, life is full of them. Two can handle these crises better than one. Ecclesiastes says, "Two are better than one, for if one falls, the other can lift them up." Why be alone when you can have someone to help and support when you need it? Unfortunately, a man will find himself alone if he verbally attacks his wife. This often leaves emotional scars, which make it difficult at best to forgive and forget.

Men, think back to when you first met the wife of your dreams. Did you use her as a guilt dump? I would say emphatically no. More than likely, you didn't see her faults and, therefore, did not pick on her regarding those faults, for you could only see the good. The good is all anyone ever sees when they first fall in love. In fact, if this initial stage of infatuation was not a part of the process, precious few relationships would ever make it to the stage of marriage. The reason is simple: you would be seeing what you don't like about the person right up front. Too soon, the don't likes would outweigh the do likes, leaving little attraction and even less desire to be married to that person. The truth is this eventually happens with all the people you meet. Familiarity breeds contempt. That is human nature.

Now that we have dealt with some of the issues men seem to have, let's discuss a few about women. When it comes to spousal interaction, both men and women can be just as harsh or in need of just as much leeway. While some men are difficult to please, some women are, as well. Each is just as guilty of using this difficulty as a bat with which to hit the other. The result of using these faults as a weapon is that the receiving spouse is never able to live up to what is expected of them. They are picked at and reminded constantly of what they have or have not done or become. Both also can be quick to correct their spouse in front of others, believing the spouse will do their best to overcome the weakness and get better. The idea is that correcting them in front of others will cause them to get better. Nothing could be further from the truth.

> **Learn to do the same thing you did with your spouse**
> **when you first met, which is to overlook their faults.**
> **Focus on only the good, believing things will work out.**

As the director of the household (ladies, please don't stop reading yet, as this is further explained in chapters 5 and 11), the husband should be leading by example. If he is demeaning and belittling, this is not setting a good example. It is actually the sign of a person with a poor self-image, as well as a lack of healthy self-esteem. A husband cutting down his wife in front of others simply to help himself feel better and look superior in the process is a quick way to a broken relationship. It also dampens or eliminates what was once a good attitude in the home by suppressing the spirit of the pacesetter of the home, the wife.

On the other hand, when the wife cuts at the husband in front of others, she is essentially taking a machete to his ego, which reduces his ability to get things done. Men by nature need an ego in order to function at their best level. What they don't need, however, is the level of ego most think to be necessary. We will talk more about this in chapter 17.

There are those women who, upon seeing in a friend's husband the characteristics they would like in their own husband, begin declaring publicly the good character of the other person's husband. Their actions usually consist of loud vocal acknowledgments, such as "I wish my husband treated me the way your husband treats you." This type of verbal jab will continue all through the night to the point it becomes uncomfortable to be around. They do this because they genuinely believe this will bring their husband around. It doesn't, and it never will.

It should be quite obvious this is not the correct spousal interaction. Correcting or belittling each other in front of your friends and family is, simply put, the worst thing you could do. You should not hang out your dirty laundry for others to see, for everyone has their own. This dirty laundry is best aired or cleaned in the privacy of one's home.

CHAPTER 3

Airing Dirty Laundry

IN CHAPTER 2 WE spoke more on the importance of correct spousal interaction, ending with the mention of airing dirty laundry. This is one of the worst things anyone could do for many reasons. Each of us has our own dirty laundry with which we should be dealing instead of associating with those who hang out their dirty laundry for all to see. Besides, for most, this is a very uncomfortable situation.

There are those, however, who enjoy looking at others' dirty laundry. As a matter of fact, some are so busy listening to and looking for the nasty aspects of others' relationships that their own laundry piles up. Unfortunately, they can't see it, but those around them do. Although they seldom share much of their own dirt, they do compare themselves with those who do, in order to bolster their feeling of superiority. As they compare, however, they expose their own laundry without realizing it.

**Don't get caught up in the dirty laundry of others, for
you will forget to wash your own.**

The problem with sharing your dirty laundry with others is that it keeps you from washing your own laundry in the privacy of your own home. Stated another way, you are not working on trying to fix the issues in your relationship. The reason for this is often simple: you don't have the time to wash it because you are too busy sharing your own dirt or listening to others share, theirs.

The thought process seems to be, 'If I air it, it will all go away'. However, the opposite is true. As a matter of fact, it will make things worse, not better. If you are going to air something, air it in your own private time of prayer and meditation, or air it to your spouse by being open and honest. And, when you do share with your spouse, do so with genuine humility and honesty instead of sharing to see if it shocks them or to see what type of reaction you can get out of them. Sharing in the correct manner allows both to know the true heart of the other.

When you or your spouse shares dirty laundry with others, the very foundation of your relationship is shaken and weakened. This is very important to understand. Doing so only bolsters the negative and thus reduces the chances of repairing what is more than likely an otherwise good relationship. It is only when information is shared in the correct manner with the right person that things can work out. Any other type of sharing can weaken and ultimately destroy the relationship. Again, this type of information should only be shared in your prayer closet or with your spouse in an open and honest manner.

It is also best to remember while in your prayer closet, it doesn't help when your prayers are cutting down or attacking your spouse. When listening to the other share their heart with you, be careful not to react with shock or astonishment. Doing so will only drive the other into silence and thus keep them from sharing anything in the future.

When I first met the girl who became my wife, upon my return home I wrote her one of many letters, sharing my innermost feelings. She didn't get the first letter for several months. From that initial letter on, I laid open my heart. My early sharing was with extreme intimidation and fear. Of all there was to fear, I was most fearful of her rejecting me, especially because I poured out my heart through the written word. The fear in me was so strong at times that it caused me to shake. Fortunately for me, the rejection never came, nor did she laugh at me. She accepted me for what and who I was at the time, which was a young man in love with a beautiful young woman who wound up becoming my best confidant and friend.

Though I know God continues to work in me, my wife's faith and belief in me is the reason I am who I am today. This angel has stood beside me through it all, and there have been some overwhelmingly tough and turbulent times, due to circumstances in our many businesses and finances and in our relationship as well.

**When your spouse shares his or her intimate thoughts
or shortcomings, it is best to be supportive rather than
reacting in shock and disgust. Allow your spouse to open
up, and together you will overcome.**

Due to her acceptance of and faith in me, I was able to share without the fear of being rejected. I shared everything with her, laying open my heart. As a matter of fact, soon after we were married, I had a few dreams of other women, which left me with a very guilty conscience. I felt I had to share this with her. In the beginning I was too afraid to share, so I kept these dreams to myself. What I know now, but didn't know then, was that keeping these dreams a secret helped them become stronger, until I didn't know what to do except confess what was happening. Interestingly enough, when I humbly shared each dream and what it was about, the dream of that particular person stopped.

It was as if the dream was getting its power from the fact that it was hidden. Solomon knew this when he wrote in Proverbs, "Forbidden bread is sweet." Once I shared what was going on with my wife, the dream lost its power and dissipated. This happened four times, and then the dreams ceased to exist. This is correct spousal interaction, for both of us did what we were supposed to do. Neither one chastised, judged, or rejected the other. By working together we were able to help me overcome what could have gotten out of control and caused us to separate.

It is important to note that having someone work with you through these uncomfortable situations in the same manner that my wife did with me is the exception, not the rule. It seems in most cases humans are very insecure; therefore, if a wife confides in her husband with such information, instead of being supportive, he flies into a jealous rage, chastising her while hating the guy. And the wife does the same. This is extremely damaging to the marital relationship and can be the cause of irreparable harm.

**Emotional and psychological insecurities are the primary
reasons for problems in the marital relationship.**

The correct response is to trust your spouse and yourself. More often than not, the one who is the most jealous is usually the one with the worse problem. Remember, emotions are to be schooled and restrained;

otherwise, uncontrollable emotions will control your life, taking you down the road to ruin. Emotions are important, emotions are good, and emotions are necessary, but they should not rule you.

Often out-of-control emotions are believed to be deep love, when in truth they are not. Out-of-control emotions are no more than a bad temper gone to seed. Real love is not based on how you feel; it is based on commitment, and for this I am thankful. If love was based simply on feelings, well, most of us would have few, if any, family or friends left after our uncontrolled emotions drove them all away.

CHAPTER 4

The Wife: The Attitude Pacesetter of the Home

CORRECT SPOUSAL INTERACTION CAN positively affect the atmosphere of the home, making it calm and inviting. Spousal interaction can negatively or positively affect the attitude and pace of the home, which are generally set by the wife.

The woman, as the attitude pacesetter, is similar to the stewardess. As a matter of fact, there was a reason airline companies chose women and not men in the beginning to be flight attendants. Women, by nature, respond to a dangerous situation with a gasp, a shriek, or a scream. However, what if the flight attendant is calm, cool, and collected? Wouldn't the passengers be, as well? It just so happens, the corporate heads of the major airline companies knew the women were the attitude pacesetters. This means they also knew that, if they could keep their cool, then everyone would believe all was okay, even though the plane was in a vertical fall and the oxygen masks were hanging down and emergency flashers were blinking. I am being facetious, but you get the point.

In most cases, the female is the attitude pacesetter of the home. Thus, when she is calm, all is calm; when she is agitated, all are agitated; and when she keeps her cool, the atmosphere around her is in the same state. Allow me to set up the typical bad-weather situation on a commercial airline. The captain gets on the PA system to let everyone know they need to stay seated, with their tray tables up, seats in the upright and locked position, and of course with seat belts fastened tight across the waist. In the meantime, the plane is shaking, bouncing, rising, and falling, while the passengers are looking out the windows, gripped with fear. The captain gets back on the PA system, admonishing the passengers to be calm, as he has everything under control. But are the passengers calm?

No, of course not! Furthermore, do they even believe what the captain is saying? No. Why? Because people know by nature how men and women react; therefore, they know it is the captain's job to tell them to be calm. The truth is they will not be calm, and most will not believe him.

If, on the other hand, a female flight attendant is calm and collected, walking the aisles and telling everyone all will be well, her very demeanor has a calming effect. The airline companies put these female flight attendants through rigorous training to ensure they do not react to the turbulence or possible disaster with fear, but remain calm, cool, and collected. They knew this would have a great effect on the passengers, as they would trust a woman, where they might not necessarily trust a man.

The reality is that people know that if a woman can maintain her calm, cool, and collected behavior, then they should be able to do the same. But a man will tell you what he wants you to hear. The scenario then would play out something like this: The female flight attendant is on the PA system, telling passengers in a calm voice that all is well (even though the plane is no longer flying in the horizontal position, but losing altitude with erratic behavior). The plane is about ten seconds from crashing, yet, instead of chaos; most of the passengers mimic the demeanor of the flight attendant, who just happens to be calm in this frightening situation.

Let me give you one other example: A husband and wife are leaving their home, heading out for an evening of fine dining. He has been gone about ten minutes when he hears that one sound that makes his heart leap into his throat: "Oh my God." The words are said with such emotion and desperation that all he can think is that she left the gas stove on under a pot, which will catch fire, or she left a candle burning on the wooden nightstand, or she saw something in the road, or she knows someone is about to pull in front of him, etc. He panics, immediately applying the brakes and nearly causing an accident as he looks around for the apparent danger. Unfortunately, the people around them have no idea what is going on. He immediately starts turning the car, nearly flipping it, because he assumes she is panicked about something at home. Meanwhile, other cars are doing their best to avoid an accident, for which he is about to be responsible.

If the wife is panicked, the house will be in a state of panic as well. The same goes for being at a restaurant, in the car, or on a plane. The attitude of a woman can instill fear or panic in the hearts of all around, while the correct attitude can inspire courage.

Later, after the accident, he is standing in front of the judge, who asks what happened. He explains, "Your Honor, we had been driving for about ten minutes, heading out for a night of fine dining—date night, if you will, Your Honor. Anyway, as I was driving, out of nowhere, with heart-gripping emotion, my wife says, 'Oh my God.' Well, sir, my heart leaped into my throat as I thought of all that could be wrong, including our house burning down or something in the road or someone about to pull in front of us. I just didn't know what was going on, as she sounded so serious, so desperate. I applied the brakes, and the car behind me had no time to respond. I saw them coming up behind, so I tried to turn out of their path to avoid being rear-ended, but they clipped the right rear of my car and pushed me into oncoming traffic. It was horrible, Your Honor. I am sorry, Your Honor, but I am grateful no one was seriously hurt."

The judge, appearing as if he is trying not to laugh, looks him straight in the eye and says, "I know exactly what you are talking about, son. I have been there myself. All men have. Seeing as how no one was seriously hurt and the insurance companies have worked out all settlements, I am going to dismiss the charges. You are free to go. You might want to get a handle on this and learn to expect this type of behavior so this doesn't happen again in the future."

What is my point? Women are the attitude pacesetters of the home and wherever they might be, such as a store, a restaurant, the car, or an airplane. When a woman panics, everyone panics—hence, airlines chose to use women who had their emotions schooled so they would not panic or react in fear. They were trained to remain calm in the face of disaster. On the other hand, men are not so much given to fear. Men are known for keeping their cool. Men are more known for schooling their emotions. Men are known for being logical, whereas women are not. More often than not, this has to do with men playing the part of being in control. As a result, they play the tough guy by keeping their emotions in check. It doesn't mean they are not afraid—more often than not they are. They are simply playing the part, and people know it.

Ladies, it may appear to you as if men are getting off scot-free, but they are not. We are about to expose some of their antics.

So what part does the husband/man play in this?

CHAPTER 5

The Influence of the Husband

What influence, if any, does the husband have on the wife, as the attitude pacesetter? If the wife's role in the home is to be the attitude pacesetter, then what is the husband's role? Why is it we are always on our best behavior in front of others and on our worst in front of our family? Which of those parties is the most important? The answer to each of these questions will help us to better understand the dynamics of the marital relationship.

It is important to understand that the behavior of the husband, as well as his treatment of his wife, has everything to do with his wife's ability to set the attitude and pace of the home. This is similar to your manager or supervisor at work belittling you, mistreating you, and generally making you miserable yet expecting you to perform at your best. This manager's bad attitude has also made for a poor working atmosphere. When you consider the husband's role as the director of the home, consider the type of director he might be or if he is directing at all.

If he is like many managers, he is loud and boisterous, using his voice and size to intimidate or threaten. He may have those in his family doing what he wants, but this does not mean he is directing. As a matter of fact, there is often no direction going on whatsoever. There are no set guidelines or boundaries, by which everyone must abide. As you delve into this a little further, you will find it a truth that many managers and husbands are not directing. They are simply employing the bully method. This method has everyone walking on eggshells, but usually only when the manager or husband is around.

As a result, the wife, realizing there has to be some form of consistent discipline, as well as guidelines and boundaries put in place, sets about to do this by taking over this important responsibility. She often does this underhandedly so as not to rock the boat or ruffle his feathers. She finds this to be much easier than the confrontation and constant fighting in front of the children.

The behavior of the husband and how he treats his wife will have a significant impact on the wife's ability to set the attitude and pace of the home.

Although the wife is at least doing something by taking matters into her own hands, what she is doing can be as damaging as what the husband is not doing. As an example, compare what the wife was doing in the home to doing the same thing in a corporate setting. What if the president was a loser and not providing any leadership? What if the vice president saw this and, as a result, began to do what the wife was doing by undermining the president? Would this be good for the company? Of course not. Could it damage the company, as well as the relationship between the president and vice president? Of course it could. Could this cause the demise of the company? It definitely could. So can what the wife is doing cause irreparable damage to her marital relationship, as well as to the entire family? Although what she is doing may not be best, she nonetheless is doing what she is doing to keep some semblance of direction and organization in the home. She is, in essence, doing what the VP might be doing if, in fact, there was no leadership in the company.

There is something else that comes to the surface in the comparison of the husband and wife with the president and vice president of a company. The husband has the ability to positively or negatively affect the wife's ability to be a good attitude pacesetter. In most corporations worldwide, there is one president, not two. On most boards, there is one chairman, not two. In war, there is one commander general, not two. This means the responsibility is on one person. Somebody has to be in charge, and somebody needs to lead and direct.

In other words, there is one head, not two. Though the human body may grow from a few pounds at birth to, as is seen in some cases, well over five hundred pounds, it doesn't mean the body needs two heads in order to properly function with a body two, three, four, or five times the normal size. The body, small or large, needs only one head. And that head needs to do its job. When the chairman, president, and general don't do their job, they are relieved of their duties and someone else is put in their place.

This may seem like an oversimplification, but nonetheless it is how it works. It is my opinion, therefore, that someone in the relationship has to be in charge; both can't lead, and both can't direct. It is also my opinion that this falls on the husband. Unfortunately, many do not wind up rising to the occasion, and in some cases they don't even try. In this case, the wife will rise to the occasion, because someone has to fill the position if anything is ever going to get started or completed.

Before I move on, there is another dynamic that is important to know. Most of us are on our best behavior around those outside our immediate family. As a result, we have a tendency to treat others better than our spouses and children. It is the natural occurrence for all to do this, believing those we love will understand and those outside the family will not.

With the above being said, I find it interesting that few take the time to think before they speak or act. They simply do, and the thinking comes later. Don't get me wrong, I must include myself in this group. Truly the majority have to be included. It is this way with both husband and wife, especially when it comes to acting or reacting in front of our families.

Remember Newton's law: every action has an equal and opposite reaction. This is what happens in our homes. We act out, and there is an "equal and opposite" reaction from our spouse and/or children. We don't like the reaction, so we act out again, and once again there is an equal and opposite reaction. This can become a vicious cycle. How we act as husbands, therefore, can determine or influence the atmosphere in the home in the same manner as the actions of the manager affect the atmosphere at an office or any place of business.

Acting and reacting cause the home to fall into a vicious cycle, for how we act determines the atmosphere in the home.

You may ask how this works if, in fact, the wife is the one setting the attitude and pace. To explain, it is necessary to talk a little about the role of the husband, the supposed director of the home. As the director, the husband is to lead and administrate. He is to see the big picture as he drives or steers the family in the direction in which they should go. If the husband is directing as he should, the wife and the children will be at ease, because the atmosphere in the home will be as it should be. The wife and children will not be anxious or worried, as they would have the confidence of knowing their director is out front, doing his best to provide for and protect them.

When a husband is fulfilling his role as director, he is also being a good leader, a good provider, a good friend, a good father, and a good husband. If he shows respect to the family, he will receive the same in return. A husband, directing as he should, makes it easy for the wife to set the correct pace of the home. When the attitude and pace are correct, the children are happy, as they grow up in the proper learning environment (i.e., Dad loving Mom, and Mom loving Dad, while both love the children).

The above, however, is not usually the case. Most husbands are insecure in many areas of their lives, so it stands to reason they would be insecure about directing the home. If they are not doing a good job of directing their own lives, how then could they be good at directing the lives of others? Being insecure makes it difficult for the husband to be a good director. This leads to other issues that carry over into all of his abilities, more importantly his ability to be a leader, as well as to be respected in his home. Because of his insecurities, he becomes agitated if questioned, often becoming angry or loud. He may roar like a lion, in hopes of letting everyone know he is king. But since he doesn't feel like a king in his heart, it will be evident to his family. The result will create and foster ill feelings, causing distance between him and his family. Much of the distance is caused by his fear of his family getting too close. He does not want them to get too close, as they would see he is not perfect. They would find out he is human, with faults, having dents in his armor. The result of this mind-set is a vicious cycle (spoken of previously), and the cycle will continue unless the husband does something to stop it.

Because of his insecurity, the husband plays the role of director by being the hard hitter around the house. His concept of directing is to act as the tough guy, thinking this is what will keep his home in line. Being firm, he demands that his family follow his directions rather than his doing what is necessary to earn their trust, respect, and support. His actions cause divisions in the home, leading to Mom protecting the children and the children protecting Mom—and doing so behind Dad's back. There is now a schism in the home.

At this point the atmosphere in the home is not one of peace or love; it is one of anxiety. Witnessing Dad's actions, Mom has been getting schooled on what to do as well as what not to do—not for the good of the family, but in order to keep Dad happy and maintain a tolerable home atmosphere.

> **Most men are insecure in many areas of their life and are, therefore, insecure about directing the home. This leads to a lack of respect from those in the home. He reacts by playing or taking on the tough-guy role, hoping to gain respect, but only gaining their fear.**

I just provided you with a description of most homes. This was my home when I grew up. My parents were not bad people; they simply had bad training (this means no training). They followed their hearts, but their hearts were misled. Their insecurities kept them from doing what was right. If the husband does not have the respect of his wife, then contrary to what he believes, he is not directing, and she is not following. And if she is not following, neither are the children. She might appear to be following, but it is in appearance only. Thus, through the behavior shown above, the husband influences the attitude and pace of the home.

It is common at this point in the relationship for the husband to become concerned about how he and his family are being perceived by those outside his home. He does his best to direct things so that those outside the home believe everything inside the home is fine. He has become good at this since he is better at showing his good side to his colleagues and those outside the home than those in the home. Those inside the home are only receiving what is left, and there isn't much. Most of the energy has been spent on the facade to all but the family. This is typical of most families, especially most husbands. What makes things worse is that we expect the family to understand this, to allow it, and to overlook it. We expect the family to say our irrational behavior is acceptable and let it go.

**Men are often more concerned with what those around
think about him and his family than he is with doing
what is right and letting it all fall into place naturally.**

The funny thing is, the irrational behavior of the others in the
home is not acceptable, at least according to Dad. On the other hand,
apparently his irrational behavior is. Really? Why is that? Why is it we
give our best to the rest of the world, and we give that which is left to
our family? Shouldn't it be the other way around? If we treated those at
home better, the world in which we live would become better overnight.
There would be fewer people getting in trouble or serving time in jail.
Unfortunately, we have been convinced that what we have been doing is
correct, even though the evidence tells a different story.

CHAPTER 6

---◈---

It All Starts at Home

IT IS MOST UNFORTUNATE how the majority of us become so concerned with what others outside of our home think of us or what might or might not be going on. What I find quite sad is that we do not seem to be as concerned with what our family thinks as much as we are with what others think. I am sure most know it would be best to be less concerned with how we look to the world and to be more concerned about how we look to our family. I am sure most of us know our family should be our first order of concern. The sad fact is, though we know this intellectually, we do not practice it in life, for it is not in our heart to do so. This is important, for when that part of our life is in order, the rest of the world falls into place.

It is time we become more concerned with what those in our home think than what those outside the home think, for our family and home life should be our first order of concern.

Because most of us are overly concerned with what others think, rather than what our families think, we have what could be viewed as an inverted pyramid. Stated another way, the base needs to be larger than the top, for a larger base makes for a stronger foundation. A small base with a larger top will cause the structure to be unstable.

It seems we spend too much time putting on a facade for others, to make sure all they see is perfect. We don't spend nearly enough time building a strong foundation for our home and marriage. What we do is similar to constructing a building but never ensuring the foundation is broad enough to carry the weight of what is being built—hence, the inverted pyramid. A little wind, a little shift of the soil, a little too much weight on the top left or top right, and the pyramid begins to lean. Eventually, there is enough outside influence to cause the pyramid to topple, which is what happens to too many marriages.

This would not happen if the pyramid is built properly. If it is built properly, the base would be larger than the top. If you invert the pyramid with the smaller portion below and the taller portion on the top, the building will be unstable. Regardless of the type of building, the taller the building, the larger the requirement for the foundation or base. As your family grows, it is important the base grows stronger as well. Just like strong winds and harsh storms test the structure of a building, your marriage and family unity will be tested as well. Unfortunately, most do not have a strong foundation and, thus, are not ready when the storms hit. And the storms hit us all.

> **Living with a facade is like building an inverted pyramid, which will soon topple. Living with a facade will cause you to be caught off guard when the tests come—and they always come.**

Just as strong winds and earthquakes test the stability of a building, heavy rains test the strength of a roof, cold and heat test the insulation factor, and so on, there will be tests against your family structure as well. For example, the time will come when someone else will lend an ear to your wife—an ear you didn't have time to give her. However, you had plenty of time to give to others, as you were more concerned about what they thought than what your wife thought. Remember, she of all people should understand, but she should not have to, for she should be your first priority.

There will be a time when what you have or have not taught your children will be compared with what they are being taught in school by teachers, by friends, and by others who are much older. They will make choices you may not agree with. There will be a time when your influence on your family—your children, in particular—will be tested by the influence of others. These tests will cause your children to question your authority. They will cause your children to question the boundaries and restrictions you have set, as well as the validity of these boundaries.

The degree to which this questioning period challenges what they have been taught at home could have been avoided or lessened had one spent the time to build and reinforce the home foundation. Unfortunately, we are not taught this at home or at school. We are not even taught this because we may happen to live in America. The truth is, your physical or geographic location doesn't matter, because it all starts with you, and it all starts at home, wherever that home is located.

> **Remember, it is always easier to influence those outside your home than those inside your home. Spend time working on and building your home life first.**

Correct spousal interaction is fundamental to a successful marriage, to successful child rearing, and to a successful home. It is even fundamental to a successful life. One may live with the appearance of success, but without a home where there is a loving spouse and children of character, any and all success is limited to you and you alone. These successes, as a matter of fact, may be held in disdain by the family, especially the children.

It is my belief that the above happens because it is often easier to influence others, because they are not as familiar with you as your family members, who know all of your quirks and idiosyncrasies. "Familiarity breeds contempt." Therefore, if you have been married for ten years and your wife still thinks you are "the man," then odds are you are doing something right. When you have been married twenty years and she feels the same, then, my friend, you are working at it. When you have been married thirty years and she still feels the same, you have the candle lit at both ends to keep the home fire burning. When you stay married for forty or fifty years, either you are still fertilizing and working on the grass at home or she has selective amnesia, which was probably brought on by hanging out or putting up with you.

> **It is often easier to sell your ideas, beliefs, and concepts to the outside world, but when those in your home are buying them, you are obviously doing something right.**

When what you do works at home, what you have is worth sharing. If it doesn't work at home, there is no value in anything you might share, as you are trying to impress rather than express. Both the wife and children know if Dad is blowing smoke, because they are familiar with the real dad, while the rest of the world—the world he is trying to impress—is not. With the outside world he can share his ideas and concepts, and by and large they are accepted. At home, however, at least for the most part, his ideas are a no-go. It is important to recognize it all starts at home.

CHAPTER 7

Familiarity Does Not Always Have to
Breed Contempt

INDEED, AS WAS PREVIOUSLY stated, it starts at home. Even Jesus understood this, for he said, "A prophet is honored everywhere except in his own town, among his own relatives and in his own home." Again, this is saying that familiarity breeds contempt. More often than not, when people are too familiar with us, they are unable to receive anything of value that we may be able to share. This can encompass wisdom or insight, direction or guidance, or even the simplest of advice. Why is it like this?

It is like this because they know us, or at least they think they do. In the case of close friends or family, they are close enough to have seen our dents, weaknesses, and faults. This, in turn, clouds their ability to believe we have anything of value to offer, which is why it is quite impressive when a wife sticks by her husband even after he makes mistakes. In most cases, she of all people truly knows him best. That being said, if a woman of character happens to believe in her husband, then it might be wise for others to do the same. When both husband and wife make their relationship their top priority, giving it their best, not what is left over, good things are always the result.

The closer people are to you, the tougher it is for them to see or believe in any innate abilities you may have.

I understand there are women who are the exceptions to this rule; they believe in their husband even when they know he is a jerk, a liar, a cheat, a thief, or a con artist. He may have even conned everyone, including her. I am not speaking of this type of woman, but rather the woman who sees beyond the fact that her husband is human. She believes he is not only capable of doing the right thing, but he is capable of doing great things. As they say, behind every great man there is a great woman. It seems this is the rule, for behind most great men there have been equally great women. It was often that great woman's belief in her husband that keeps him going when the going gets tough.

My own personal experience has proven this to be true. During my early twenties I was overwhelmed, and life seemed too tough. It seemed life wasn't worth the battle, and it was becoming hard to continue. I often felt I could not go on. Instead of calling me a loser and putting me down, my wife got behind me and pushed, or she got in front and pulled. She did whatever she could to prod me on, not allowing me to quit. When I felt like a total failure, she was there by my side, shoring me up. She was my coach and my cheering squad. She knew what was in me; therefore, she worked with me until that which was on the inside worked its way to the outside. The results of this collaboration and support were, in the long run, best for us both. I grew, she grew, and together we formed a master mind that has been very successful. It has been severely tested, but it has been successful.

A good spouse can become your coach and/or cheering squad.

For the man of the house, the challenge is to direct and lead in spite of his shortcomings, in spite of the dents in his armor, and in spite of his weaknesses and faults. In order to do this, he is challenged to get back in the car even after driving it into the ditch. He is challenged to get back on the right road, even when in the past he had chosen, against the wishes of his wife, the wrong road. He is challenged to continue on the path even though the going is tough.

This is where the college of life comes into play. Children and others will, through observance, learn how to act when times get tough or things go wrong. They will learn what to do should they take the wrong road or make the wrong decisions. They will learn, although a mistake is made, it can be made better, when their response is proper. In short, what they have witnessed by watching Dad and Mom work through the issues together is what will make them a success too.

It is better to offer verbal and physical support than utilizing the phrase "I told you so" as a means of elevating yourself while belittling your spouse.

Allow me to digress a moment to talk about choosing to take a road against the wishes of your wife. There may be only one or two things that can cause humility to a greater degree than when a husband's disagreement with his wife winds up leading both to failure or shipwreck. As horrible as this seems, it can become a learning moment for both. Although the husband is not always right, someone has to be able to break the tie when there is a disagreement. It is my belief God has placed this ultimate responsibility on the husband, even though at times he is not so good at directing and even though he might make a lot of mistakes. What will happen if they both respond properly? Things will work out for the best in the end.

Allow me to give you an example: It is common for women to have a great memory—or, as it is called, the memory of an elephant—with the ability to recall anything that has happened as far back as she has known you. Women also have a tendency to be "I told you so" responders. This means that when they disagree with you, but you head in your direction anyway and you fail, they will often walk right up to you and let you know all about how you failed. It can play out like this: You disagree on what road to take, so you decide to take the one you were sure was right. You head down the road and crash into the ditch. The car lands on your side, with your door crushed into the wall of the ditch, leaving you unable to open the door or release your jammed seat belt.

Learn to be a supporter of your spouse, not a detractor. As a detractor, you wind up belittling yourself, as you chose to be with this person.

Your wife, on the other hand, is on the upside. Her door is not damaged, so it can open. Her seat belt is not stuck, so she is able to get out. What she could do (and in most cases does) is look over at you and say, "I told you so, but you wouldn't listen. I told you the other way was best, but, no, we had to go your way." On the other hand, she could free herself, get out of the car, and call for help. By doing this she is simply offering you a helping hand, never mentioning what just happened. Oh, she will be tempted to do so, but not doing so will put both of you back on the road to your destination, and oddly enough you may even wind up getting there quicker than you might have had you taken the right road from the start.

Why is this? Well, all I can say is it seems we are all placed in these learning moments to test our response to the situation and help us learn. The correct response determines how we come out on the other side. Remember, correct spousal interaction is what will bring a better tomorrow. Better tomorrows do not come about by trying to take back what has already been said or done; they only come when we do that which will bring them about, which is the correct spousal interaction.

CHAPTER 8

I Told You So

THE MAJORITY OF US will wind up in the "I told you so" column. Most husbands and wives succumb to the pressure, unable to let the mistake go by without using that very phrase. When the spouses cannot agree on which road to take, and the husband decides to go his route instead of taking her route, there is great potential for use of the phrase "I told you so." Whether the wife decides to get in the car with him or not, there will more than likely be ample occasion for her to rub it in, if she so desires. Even if she had to climb out of the car or simply watched him drive into the ditch, there will be opportunity for both to work together to get through this incident correctly and back on the road to their intended destination.

I believe I am most fortunate in that my wife has never played the "I told you so," card, even when both she and I knew my decision was based solely on spite rather than common sense. There I went, driving down the road, just to prove I was the one in charge, only to wind up driving into the ditch. Still, although she believed me to be incorrect, she climbed in and off we would go, down the wrong road. Then, after the crash, she climbed out the window and offered a helping hand, never once saying, "I told you so." Before you run off thinking it only happens with the husband, believe me, it works both ways. More often than not, however, I believe it should be the husband making the final decision. I know some men don't make decisions, leaving them to the wife, and we will get to that in chapter 10.

**When you respond in the right manner, this seldom gives
your spouse an opportunity to place the blame on you,
leaving them to feel they are right.**

At times it might have helped me if she had used the "I told you
so" phrase, for then I could have argued my way out of the feeling of
worthlessness and failure. What I am saying is I could have used the
argument to turn the whole thing around and place the blame on her.
Or at least I could have tried. But alas, I was not given the chance. I was
allowed to seethe in my own thoughts, as she permitted me to deal with
it alone. The whole time she supported our combined efforts to get the
truck back onto the right road. Soon, we were at the destination both
had desired. Truth be told, I was beating myself up badly enough. Had
we entered into an argument, this would have given me a way out of
having to think about my poor choice and failure, as it would have been
necessary to put this aside in order to come out on top of the argument.
That is what men do, right? They make sure they come out on top. I
would not call this the correct spousal interaction. We will talk about this
a little more in chapter 9 as well.

I am searching for the words to explain how difficult it is not to play
the "I told you so" card. By using the term, we might feel better for the
moment. We might even have proven our point. We might have won
that round. But we will not have bettered our marriage or strengthened
our bond. We will have thrown a rock, which would inevitably leave an
emotional scar. We can't take back the spoken words, which likely take
deep root in the heart, causing separation on an intellectual, emotional,
and physical level. The scar will be seen each time you look in the mirror.

How and why will this scar be seen? Well, the answer is simple.
Because you were the brunt of what was said, looking in the mirror
provides a reflection of what was said about you. Each look in the mirror
may continue to deflate your ego, self-image, and confidence. In any case,
your relationship will be adversely affected and severely strained. It will
remain so, until the one wronged forgives the one doing the wrong, even
if the one doing the wrong never apologizes. It takes a mature and strong
person to overcome a derogatory comment, and we must overcome in
order to move forward with a productive life.

Allowing those who have made mistakes to deal with them on their own, without your interference, is often harder than providing them an out by giving them a reason to argue.

As for having to win simply because you are the man of the house, this will depend on your definition of winning. Winning isn't always about you being on top or having things come out the way you preferred. I am speaking to men here, but this can apply to both husband and wife. What this is really about is directing and leading the home and doing so in a manner that encourages the family to respect your decisions. It is not so that you will look good in front of others, nor is it in order for you to feel superior all the time, which is usually why men do it. It is for the betterment of all in the family, not just you.

The husband should do what is necessary to make his family better, even if it requires self-debasement. This is not the attitude of most husbands, for most will sacrifice their families to look good in front of those around them. A true leader will make sure those he is directing look the best, because when they do he is doing his job correctly. He will receive all of the credit necessary through the validation of a successful marriage, a great family, and a good home.

When my wife and I were first married, friends said I was making a mistake by putting her before them and making her my best friend. Instead of spending time with them hunting, shooting, camping, fishing, or playing sports, I chose to hang out with her. Rather than going off and playing handball with the guys or challenging the best players, I chose to play handball with her. Believe me, this was not easy. I was an excellent player who was now playing with someone who offered no challenge. It was difficult at first, but I soon learned this helped us to grow together.

Winning isn't always being on the top of the heap. When it comes to the spouse and family, winning means everyone in the family benefits, not just you.

By spending time with her I was learning patience as well as gaining knowledge about how we responded to each other as we interacted. I began to learn many things about her, including how she would react under pressure and in competition. Had I been concerned about how I looked solely to my friends, I don't believe our relationship would be what it is today. By choosing to spend time with her rather than concerning myself about how I looked to the guys, I allowed the two of us to build a good foundation, which has now lasted many years.

CHAPTER 9

---◈---

The Need to Win

THE NEED TO WIN, though predominant in males, can be a female issue as well. Some women, like most men, just can't stand to lose; therefore, they will do whatever it takes to win, even if it means throwing the husband under the bus. Most of us have been subjected to the jabs between spouses when we are out with them for an evening or spending a few days with them, and to most of us, these situations are very uncomfortable.

The interaction often starts out innocent, but if one of them has been wronged earlier in the day or even earlier in the week, this will soon come out in their conversation. You will know for certain whether one is still angry or has let it go and forgotten it. This will become apparent when, for instance, they see an opportunity to better themselves or one-up the other by making the other look bad and, more often than not, they take it. The result of these skirmishes never winds up good for the participants or the spectators. As a spectator, this can be very uncomfortable. It is not something most choose to be around. My wife and I certainly do not.

**Too often in our effort to win, we step on others to
elevate ourselves.**

The scene usually plays out as follows: One begins to tell a story, but the other keeps butting in and correcting them. The one initiating the story does their best to complete it, but the other continues to say it didn't happen that way. Soon, there are cutting little comments, such as "Oh, come on, it didn't happen like that at all." Or "Oh no, that is not how it happened at all. It actually went down like this . . ." Then "Why are you making up stuff?" Or "Speaking of that, you know what the idiot did this week? Talk about stupid, he is about as stupid as one could be. I can't believe I married that moron." Then "You don't know the half of it. Living with him is like living in hell." And finally, "Can you believe anyone can be as dumb as he is?"

When these types of comments are thrown around, they can, like rocks, leave scars. Such comments do not promote healthy relationships through proper communication, nor are they uplifting or encouraging.

The scarring often remains in our hearts or is worn on our faces, or both, until we visit the plastic surgeon of forgiveness. It is only forgiveness that will remove these scars from our face and heart. Without the surgery of forgiveness, the haunting memory will always be there to take us back to that which caused the scarring.

Cutting comments toward anyone can leave scars in their heart if the comments are not dealt with properly.

I offer a suggestion of help here. Though scars might remind you of where you have been, they don't have to dictate where you are going. Where you are going is your choice to make. Do not allow what others have done to you to determine how your tomorrows will turn out. When you harbor bitterness, anger, and hatred, those with whom you are angry will be the ones dictating where you go and what you do. It will happen by default.

If winning is your ultimate goal (and it should be), make sure what you are winning is what will bring you the reward you seek. If I am to win at being a father, I will need to become the type of father it takes to make that happen. I will need to be honest with my children. I will need to share the many mistakes I have made as well as what I did to correct and overcome them. I need not be so quick to condemn for the mistakes they make. I need to allow enough leeway for them to know there is room to right the wrong. I need to learn how to communicate the detriment of condemnation rather than allow it to direct them in a life of guilt. Traveling this road will keep them going in circles, and they will not be free to grow or achieve. They will be bound by their faults and shortcomings as they travel the vicious cycle of defeat and despair. That is not winning.

**Do not allow what others have done to you to be seen on
your face or remain in your heart.**

If I am to win at being a good husband, then I shouldn't require more of my wife than I do of myself. This seems to be the issue in many cases. For example, it is often okay for the husband to make a mistake, but not for the wife. It is often okay for the parent to make a mistake, but not for the child. There seems to be a double standard by which the husband lives.

If I am to win as a husband, then it has to start with me. I have to become what it takes to set the right example. If we are to win as a family, then the husband has to be involved as well. The wife cannot do it alone, which it seems is most often the case. This requires the husband to give 110 percent to his relationship with his spouse and children. The husband must buy into the concept of accepting nothing less than becoming what it takes to be a winning husband, leader, and director of the home.

CHAPTER 10

Who's Making the Decisions?

WHEN IT COMES TO decision making, it seems most wives wind up as the decision makers in the home due to the procrastination of the husbands. It simply takes him too long to make a decision. Since a decision has to be made, it falls on the only one left to make it: the wife.

If you want to see an example of how a husband's decision making/ directorship works in the family environment (not necessarily the way it works at the office), then follow him and his family to a restaurant. The husband will have one child hanging on him as he walks toward the door, while the wife will have two children dogging her. The husband will open the door for everyone, but the reason is not as it seems. He wants the wife to go in first so she can give the name and head count to the hostess while he looks around the restaurant, checking things out.

> **Too often men procrastinate in decision making, so**
> **by default the wife winds up making the decisions and**
> **taking over the leadership.**

There could be a friend or colleague or someone he might know, and he needs to make a good impression. This isn't necessarily what would be seen as being a good director or leader. Meanwhile, the children—at the very least there is always one—are running around the restaurant, looking for trouble. All of a sudden you hear a big crash of dishes, along with some oohs and aahs from those around the site of the crash.

In just a short minute or two, the manager walks over with the child responsible for the disaster, asking both parents to please watch over their children. With a quick glance, you see the child is crying, with food on his/her clothes, arms, face, and hair. All of a sudden righteous indignation rises up in the husband as he turns to tell Mom she needs to get her kids in line. Her kids? What father would say that? Well, that would be me and most of the other men I know. He then tells the children to straighten up and sit down.

The questions to ask are as follows: Where was he prior to the incident? Why is it the mother's fault? How come Dad wasn't leading when they walked in? Why didn't he have control before they entered the restaurant?

If he was truly directing, he would have opened the door for his wife and children, they would have entered, and then he would have instructed all of them to wait in the reception area while he walked ahead to the host desk to give his name and count. He would then turn around, walk back to the family to gather up at least one of the children, and direct everyone to sit down and relax for a few minutes until the table was ready. Additionally, he could have taken the restless one outside in order to contain the collateral damage. This describes a director, for this is how one makes decisions properly, as the need arises. Somehow this doesn't seem to happen. This is obviously not correct spousal interaction.

Here is another example: Both are shopping at Costco, Sam's Club, or other membership-based, large warehouse-type stores, where one can purchase mass quantities for much less than at a conventional store. These are the places you go when there is a need to purchase six pounds of cheese as well as enough lettuce for a small restaurant. While shopping, the wife asks the husband what he would like for dinner. Being the responsible party, knowing dinner will be here soon, she is thinking ahead so as not to wind up at dinnertime with nothing to eat.

The wife has had to prepare in this manner her whole married life, as the children don't care whether or not Mom and Dad are full, hungry, or sick. They don't care whether Mom and Dad don't want to think about eating, because their stomachs tell them they are hungry and thus they want to eat. So the wife is conditioned to think ahead and make decisions, whether she feels like it or not. Besides, if dinnertime comes around and there is no food on the table, how would most husbands respond? Most husbands would not be happy and would comment under their breath about Mom having nothing for them to eat. By the way, didn't she just ask him earlier what he wanted and he never answered?

Parents in general—and husbands in particular—often respond to a misbehaving child or the constant nagging questions asked by a child according to their level of inconvenience, not based on that which would been best for the child or the family at that time.

This very thing happens at our home. It is not uncommon for my wife to ask me right after we finish eating breakfast or lunch what I want for dinner. My thought, of course, is You have to be kidding me. You are thinking about dinner? That is hours away. Although it is hours away, the wife knows dinner is truly right around the corner and someone has to do the planning; otherwise it will never get done. It certainly isn't going to get done by hubby, at least in the majority of cases. If most guys are like me, they would say, "Well, I have put in my time already. I have worked a full eight-hour day and don't want to think about it or make any more decisions."

Husbands often have a tendency to procrastinate, while wives and mothers cannot afford this luxury—that is, if the house is to be kept a home.

Unfortunately, the wife doesn't usually get this luxury, and in many cases she has a full-time job. So the wife, though working a full-time job, takes care of the laundry, cooking, food purchasing, household purchases, etc. She also handles most of the issues with the children, as well as getting them ready for school. While Daddy is acting whiny and selfish, she also has the full-time job of taking care of him and making him happy. Wow, what a lucky lady she is. Not!

As odd as it seems, the above describes the woman spoken of in the Book of Proverbs, who is called the virtuous woman. She is the one who

- sets the attitude and pace of the home;
- burns the midnight oil;
- plans for and organizes most home activities;
- keeps things in check around the house;
- makes sure everything is in order;
- sees to it all are fed and clothed;
- works diligently with her hands;

- makes wise purchases as the good money manager;
- is kind to those in need;
- opens her mouth to speak with wisdom;
- does not eat the bread of idleness; and
- is spoken of highly by her children, husband, and husband's friends and colleagues.

It appears that many decisions are made by the wife on a daily basis. It also appears that the majority of these decisions are not subject to the approval of the husband, but are made through necessity to ensure a well-run household. When there is correct spousal interaction, this is exactly how things work, and it works well.

This decision making, however, is different from the type of decisions being made because of a lack of directorship and leadership by the husband. The type spoken of above comes with being the attitude and pacesetter of the home and a virtuous woman. The above is a picture of my wife for which I am grateful. I hope it is yours as well.

When the husband is doing what he needs to do as the director and leader, the wife is at liberty to set the attitude and pace of the home. When he does his thing at work and leaves it there, not bringing it home to rehash it with the family, then the wife and children are not walking on eggshells. The spirit of the house is invigorating, for they are not afraid of stepping on Dad's toes or wondering if he is in a bad mood.

CHAPTER 11

Another Way to Submit

THERE IS ANOTHER WAY a wife can deal with her husband's extremely slow or nonexistent decision making. As previously stated, it is my belief the husband, as the director of the home, should be the final decision maker. Unfortunately, many husbands never rise up to fill the position. In fact, if you follow the entire process with regard to the steps the husband would need to take to rise up to this position, you would see it starts appropriately with the husband loving his wife unconditionally.

Submission to a director or leader is easy when it is someone who has earned the privilege.

In the Bible, the husband is told five times to love his wife unconditionally. On the other hand, in the Bible, the wife is only told to love her husband one time, and this is with a fondness or as two people with common interests. The wife is also told to submit to her husband as unto the Lord; however, this submission is to someone who has earned this place of respect as well as gained a place of confidence in her heart.

I can hear the wheels turning and see the smoke coming out of the ears of many ladies, but give me a chance to explain. It truly is easier to submit when the one you submit to has earned your respect, for you will know their decisions are for the best of all, not just for themselves. On the other hand, when experience has shown the husband to be a procrastinator or an ineffective leader or director, then someone has to start making decisions in order to keep the household moving forward; hence, the wife steps up and fills the position.

If, on the other hand, the husband loves unconditionally, then he is doing his level best to earn the respect of his wife and children. Loving unconditionally is a no-conditions, no-favors-required, and no-strings-attached form of love. There should never be strings attached to why or when you love someone. This kind of love is given to the other person regardless of the circumstance. It is given regardless of their behavior, bad or good. To love in this manner takes tremendous effort, for it is not based on how you feel at any given time; it is based on a commitment, and that commitment is without any attached conditions.

A husband who loves unconditionally is going to do his level best to earn the respect of his wife and children.

In order for this to happen, one must give all they have, and it must be their best. When one is doing their best, they do not have the tendency to procrastinate. Procrastination not only reveals selfishness, but it reveals the love to be conditional. As a procrastinator, it is not be possible for a husband to fill the position of leader or director. If the husband is not leading or directing, why should the wife submit to him?

One may argue this is a biblical requirement, with God requiring that it is done in the same manner we are told to love and honor our parents even though they have not earned it. By following this example, we are putting into play that which maintains a sense of order similar to when you respect your elders, or those in law enforcement, or the leaders of your country.

When a husband is not doing a good job of leading and directing and, by default, the wife has to take the leadership role and make the decisions, I have a suggestion that just might rectify this issue altogether. Women, I suggest putting your husband in a place where it forces him to either make a decision or continue to get hit in the face with the consequences of his procrastination.

How can you do that? It is simple. Just duck. I know this sounds funny, but allow me to explain. Most often when the husband is a procrastinator and puts off making important decisions (or any decisions), the wife, by default, winds up making the decisions. If she doesn't, not one thing gets done. When she is making the decisions, she is the one feeling the brunt of everything coming down the pike, because she is the one dealing with it. This is the result of her getting tired of waiting for decisions to be made. She has learned firsthand how the wait has been a costly one for the entire family. They have paid emotionally as well as financially. Hence, she gets tired of waiting and simply takes on the responsibility.

It is best for wives to duck rather than take on the responsibility, which the husband should be carrying. It is the simplest way to submit.

I believe there is a way to get out of this position gracefully by allowing the husband to take back this leadership role. I also believe following his methodology will cause him to want that position of leadership back in order to avoid the pain you are going to enable him to feel. My suggestion is simple. To get the husband back out front and making decisions, the easiest thing to do is duck. It is that simple. Just duck.

Instead of the wife making the next decision when it comes down the road, the wife will duck down and let it pass over her head, thus hitting her husband in the face. Some husbands are quick learners and only need to be hit in the face once, while others are a bit slower with it, taking two or three hits to the face.

The caveat here is there are those deadbeat husbands who believe if they simply do nothing, you will eventually stop trying to get them to take it back. As a matter of fact, they are counting on it. Unfortunately for the most part, these husbands are incorrigible.

However, in most cases the husband will ask his wife to step aside while he "gets back up front," taking the leadership role he should never have given. This allows the wife to get back to her job of setting the attitude and pace of the home. As a result, the atmosphere of the home is much more harmonious.

Unfortunately, to get their husbands to lead or direct, most wives coerce, coax, whine, or nag. This does not work. It may appear to at first, but any results will only be short-lived. The duck method is much more effective and simpler. Most men do not like being blindsided, so when they get hit in the face a few times, they will take the necessary steps to make sure it doesn't happen again. The next thing you know he will be up front.

The standard approach most wives take to get their husbands to direct is to coerce, coax, whine, or nag. This seldom, if ever, works.

It is important to understand that a husband will not get out front if he happens to believe you are only being lazy. This will not be enough of a motivator to change him. He will only move out front and take his rightful position when he gets tired of paying the price for your laziness. In other words, if you are not doing what he thinks you should be doing—thus, causing him to suffer the consequences—he will take action.

As a result, his thoughts will turn to the idea of moving up to the front, where he can see, as well as avoid this facial assault. Hidden in these facial assaults are the responsibilities with which he should be dealing. When he properly responds, both parties wind up where they were meant to be all along. This method is flawless.

I am not saying the wife is not as good at making decisions as the husband. I am also not implying the wife is incapable of leading or directing, for our history books and the Bible tell us differently. There are thousands of historical and modern factual stories of great female leaders. Some of the most famous are Marie Curie, Susan B Anthony, Mother Teresa, Indira Gandhi, Golda Meir, Margaret Thatcher, Joan of Arc, Catherine the Great, and Benazir Bhutto. The list is endless.

It is quite obvious women are not only capable of leading, but they make good leaders when they have to step up and do the job. A good mother and wife is already a good leader, for the sign of a great leader is a great follower. Those who become the greatest at multitasking in the world are, by natural occurrence, women. Further, to be a good leader one must be good at handling multiple tasks at a time. A good mother has that going for her already; therefore, this isn't something most women have to learn. On the other hand, it does seem to be something men have to learn or, in many cases, be pushed into.

History shows us women are capable of leading and directing. Very few men, however, are capable of taking care of the home.

From the beginning, it appears God knew husbands would have a problem providing leadership and direction. In Genesis 2:24, God said, "Therefore, shall a man leave his father and mother and cleave unto his wife and they shall be one flesh." So it seems God saw many husbands just might have an issue with being out front. As a result, husbands need to be told to leave the leadership of Dad and Mom. Notice the wife is not told to do a thing, only the husband.

I believe the reason for this can be seen in a scene played out in Genesis 3, where the serpent is tempting Eve to eat the forbidden apple. Two things do not readily appear to us when we read this chapter. The first thing we see is Adam showing a lack of leadership, for it says Eve turned and gave to Adam, who was there with her. He was there the entire time, yet he never protested or tried to sway or guide her in a better direction. The second thing we see is Adam's inability to take responsibility for his actions, or lack thereof, and his underhanded way of blaming others for what happened.

Later, God came looking for Adam, but he was hidden. When God asked why he was hidden, Adam said it was because he was naked. When God asked how he knew he was naked and if he ate the apple, Adam's response was to place the blame on others. Notice, he did not place the blame on himself. He said, "It was the woman you gave to be with me." Here we see he blamed the woman first and God second.

He didn't blame himself, although he was there. He didn't admit to having provided no direction or leadership. He didn't admit to his undermining scheme of using Eve as a patsy. He had set her up to do the supposed evil deed, making it look as if it was all her idea, when in truth he knew what would happen and had planned on it happening just like it did. By using her, he was able to look good while shifting the blame and guilt to not only her, but ultimately God.

It is not because a woman isn't capable of leading, for it is quite obvious she can. It isn't because a man isn't capable of leading, because he can. What we see from the example above is Adam, the husband, did not provide leadership or direction to protect his wife, Eve. He basically threw her under the bus. Most women would not do such a thing to anyone, let alone their husband. Most women would protect their husband, even if doing so would bring hurt upon their own person, but this does not seem to be the character of all husbands.

**A good wife and mother is also a good leader. The sign of
a great leader is the ability to follow as well as multitask.
All good leaders must be able to multitask. Women do it
naturally, while most men have to work at it.**

The husband and wife were to become one flesh; therefore, they should have talked this through and worked out the solution together. Had there been a disagreement as to what direction to go in, Adam would have had the responsibility of making the final decision, but it would have been a decision that was best for both. Adam didn't choose this route. As a result, God has required all husbands to love unconditionally. God wanted to make sure men were not going to choose for themselves, as Adam clearly did. God also required that husbands take on the role of director and leader as well as own up to their mistakes, accepting their own guilt. This is not something most men do. As a matter of fact, most are quick to cast guilt and blame on everyone but themselves, as men are, for the most part, the best at setting blame.

If the husband loves unconditionally, and if he accepts his role of director and admits to his own guilt, any wife would find it is easier to submit to this type of leadership, knowing it is for the best of all involved. However, when the husband is a procrastinator, there is something the wife can do: duck. This allows the responsibilities coming down the path to hit him in the face. After a couple times, he will likely take his rightful position.

CHAPTER 12

─────◈─────

Men Have Three Basic Weaknesses: Money (Part 1)

CORRECT SPOUSAL INTERACTION IS most essential when it comes to helping the husband deal with his three basic weaknesses. It is true, both wives and husbands have weaknesses, and as such, both need to work on them; however, it is easier to work on them together. Unfortunately, the one thing the husband needs to do is also the one thing he avoids: working on his weaknesses with his wife.

> **Overcoming a weakness is no different from overcoming challenges; however, challenges are easier to overcome with the force of two rather than all alone.**

Can these weaknesses be overcome without the help of the other? Yes, they can, but this is the exception and not the rule. As a couple, there is the opportunity to form a powerful master mind, which is essentially two (or more) people pulling together in one direction. By working together they are not simply gaining the strength of two, but multiplying this many times over. The reward of working together is that the husband's three basic weaknesses can be kept in check so as not to adversely affect the marriage, the home, and his life in the long run.

Ask any woman if she thinks men have weaknesses, and she will tell you men, in general, have plenty of them. Oddly enough, men can be so strong in some areas yet be such babies when they don't feel well. The truth is most men are whiners; even the common cold, a splinter, or a hangnail can wipe them out, let alone the flu or pneumonia. On the other hand, a wife and mother usually work through all of these challenges. It is not that they are tougher; it is simply because there is no alternative. If she doesn't do it, it is not going to get done. The husband, on the other hand, has one of the best reasons for him to opt out: his wife.

Men are usually the opposite of women, and this can be of help to both in their personal development and in overcoming personal weaknesses.

If you were to ask a group of women to name the three basic weaknesses of men, the answers would be all over the map, and the list would not be limited to three; it would be quite a bit longer. This is because, as seen above, men have a tendency to whine even though they are only suffering from the common cold; therefore, this is a weakness. Men are not usually good at multitasking, or at least in most cases it does not come naturally like it does for most women—another weakness. Men are not usually patient by nature—another weakness. Men do not usually communicate well, at least to their wives. Or put differently, they don't talk or communicate when they should. This is another weakness. Men are loners by nature, and to women this is a definite weakness. Most men do not like to shop. I cannot stand to shop, and when I have to I am quick to purchase what I want, asking no questions and moving on. In the eyes of most women, this is another weakness.

With the correct spousal interaction, the wife can play a key role in helping the husband become a success.

Although there are many weaknesses that could be listed, there are three basic weaknesses that are fundamental to all men. Not all suffer the same weaknesses in all areas, yet most men have weaknesses in these three areas. A perceptive wife can help keep these in check. The correct spousal interaction will have a positive effect on not only the husband but also on the marriage and home as well. In other words, the wife has the opportunity to play a key role in helping the husband become a success. As they say, "behind every good man is a great woman."

An astute wife can help to bring a sense of balance and equilibrium into all three areas.

The three basic weaknesses of which I speak are money, sex, and ego. There is no other time that correct spousal interaction is as important as when it is applied in these three areas. An astute wife can help bring a sense of balance and equilibrium to all three areas. She can help just enough in each area so as not to overrun or impose, but enough nonetheless to leave him thinking he has it all in control. Eventually, he will come to know it is working well because of the correct spousal interaction between him and his wife. A wife's correct response to her husband's incorrect actions will bring balance. Further, the husband's correct response to the wife's incorrect actions will do the same.

Remember, opposites attract. Usually, if the husband has a type A personality, then the wife is much more passive and laid-back. And if the wife has a type A personality, the husband is passive. If the wife has a tendency to talk and interact, most men think it is too much, and then the husband is usually not as talkative. If the wife likes to shop, the husband more than likely hates shopping. As an example, my legs start hurting when my wife simply mentions shopping. As I stated before, I don't like to shop. If and when I shop, it is to find and purchase. I don't spend a lot of time shopping, for I simply see what I want, purchase it, and leave.

On the other hand, my wife loves to shop. Most would call her a professional shopper. This is not because she spends a lot of money, but because she is thrifty, always saving money. The issue I have is that it will take hours for her to find something. I, on the other hand, don't have the inclination or care, let alone the time or patience, to spend even a small portion of the time she does shopping.

If the wife likes to join groups, the husband usually likes to be alone. If the wife likes to spend money, the husband usually likes to save. If the husband is conservative, then the wife is often liberal. On the other hand, if the wife has an interest in obtaining affluence, the husband will often do whatever it takes to make her happy, as this is part of the passion driving him to please her. If the husband has a high sex drive, then the wife more than likely is not as sexually driven. If the husband has a big ego, it is not usually the case with the wife.

**A husband's three basic weaknesses can be his Achilles'
heel, but a wise wife can help him to keep these areas in
line so the power behind his passion stays focused on the
right, rather than the wrong, things.**

It is one or more of these three weaknesses that is usually the cause of
the man's downfall. These three weaknesses are often man's Achilles' heel,
but the wife can be a big help in keeping him in line so the power behind
his passion is focused on the right, rather than the wrong, things.

CHAPTER 13

Men Have Three Basic Weaknesses: Money (Part 2)

THE FIRST OF THE three basic weaknesses we shall cover is money. Money is an interesting study. Although it is an inanimate object that has no power in and of itself, we seem to give it all the power necessary to rule or even ruin our lives when we make it the focal point of our passion. Sadly, most never come to understand that money is simply a tool. It is no different from any other tool one would use to obtain what they want. A carpenter uses his hammer, saw, and levels to trade for money, food, clothing, or shelter, yet his tools are not the end-all of his passion in the manner in which people have made money the end-all of their passion.

Though an inanimate object, money seems to control the very lives of the majority and is often instrumental in the destruction of a marriage.

A wise carpenter could save much of the money he makes from his job as a carpenter and then, after gaining some financial skills, use his money as a tool in the same manner he used his carpentry tools, to make more money. Some people have more tools than others because they are more skilled at using each tool, while some are less skilled in the handling of a particular tool and it shows. I speak of the management and handling of money and each dollar being a tool.

Napoleon Hill's Think and Grow Rich appears to be an entire book about money. Upon reading, however, one will find the book is much different from what most would imagine, especially considering the title of the book. The book is not as much about money as it is about understanding the process of becoming what it takes to attract money, to make money, and most importantly to keep money. It is about becoming the person who, through proper thinking, gains the ability to use his or her intellect to focus his or her passion in the direction necessary to make and keep money. As a matter of fact, his book can be summed up in one statement: success is to be attracted by the person you become.

Money should not be the end-all of one's passion. It has no creative powers in and of itself. The power money is given resides only in you.

As a side note, there is a chapter in Hill's book called "The Mystery of Sex Transmutation," which, because of the way I was raised, I didn't read for almost ten years. For some reason, having read the rest of the book several times and finding it to be incredibly well written, I apparently did not believe this chapter would be of value. When I finally did read it, I found I had overlooked the one key ingredient that seemed to be missing from the book.

In that chapter, Hill points out the process of changing or transferring one element or energy into another—hence, transmutation. The word "sex" brings the majority of us to a certain frame of mind. Because of ignorance, as well as unsophisticated thinking, the mind-set more often than not is about physical sex or the act of making physical love. There is so much, however, that is behind sex transmutation, for it is the switching of the mind from thoughts of immediate physical expression and gratification to focused thoughts of another nature.

To paraphrase from the transmutation chapter, for certain people, sex is the most powerful human desire. When impassioned or enflamed, people are driven by this desire to develop keenness of imagination, courage, willpower, persistence, and a creative ability previously unknown to them. So strong and impelling is the drive for sexual contact that men will freely run the risk of life and reputation to indulge it. When harnessed and redirected, however, this motivating force maintains all of its attributes of keenness of imagination, courage, etc., which may be used as a powerful creative force in such things as literature, art, science, or any other profession or calling.

**Sex is the strongest of passions and human desires; it is
the strongest of drives, especially in men. Transmuting
this passion and power can help change your world and
the world of others as well.**

Hill goes on to say that the average age of those men who finally become financially successful is forty-six. Previous to this age, most men are unable to focus on the right thing, as they are not thinking with the proper organ given by God to run this body: the brain. Hill goes on to say the men of greatest achievement have always been men of highly sexed natures who learned the art of sex transmutation. He also said those who have accumulated great fortunes or achieved outstanding recognition in literature, art, architecture, or any other profession have all been motivated by the influence of a woman. How interesting. Women influence a man's decisions for bad or for good.

An example of a bad influence is Bonnie, of the infamous Bonnie and Clyde duo. What if Bonnie had not found the same excitement in stealing and running from the law? What if she had decided she did not want what that kind of money could buy? We might have had a different ending, at least one without her death and maybe without his as well. But alas, this was not to be, for the love of money was the driving force, so much so that the love of money was greater than the love of their fellow man. They did not transmute their passion for money into a love of accomplishment or achievement. They were not interested in whether all were going to win; they were interested only in the two of them winning the object of their desire: money. Most often in such cases, all wind up losing. This is always a recipe for disaster.

**Due to the strength of this passion for sexual contact,
men seldom become truly successful until the average age
of forty-six. This is because they are not thinking with
their brain, but with their sexual desire.**

The book Think and Grow Rich is not as much about money as it is about becoming successful at whatever gift or skill one may have or need to cultivate. Likewise, the chapter on sex transmutation is not as much about sex as it is about learning to focus your most powerful weapon, passion, toward something of lasting virtue.

That something of lasting value is not money. It is about focusing your passion on becoming what it takes to attract what you need and want. It is about achieving your goals and dreams and doing it via the same system available to all on this planet: attracting what you need and want by what you become. Attracting what one needs is a system whereby everyone benefits. It isn't the type of system where others cheated, ripped off, or tramped on for one's personal gain. This is the best system, yet there are always those who want to circumvent this system, but the result always leads to heartache.

CHAPTER 14

Men Have Three Basic Weaknesses: Money (Part 3)

MEN BY NATURE ARE driven to accomplish; therefore, to stir a man's passion without the ability to direct it could be setting oneself up for undesirable consequences. In the Bible, Solomon was said to be the wisest and wealthiest man to have ever lived. He wrote about the love of two people. He writes about not stirring up his love until the timing is right or until both are ready. That means not stirring up his love until maturity has been reached in thought and spirit, thereby allowing the passion to be properly directed.

Uncontrolled and misdirected passion is what leads to rape and other ungodly and immoral acts of hatred and violence. What is most important is harnessing the power and energy and thus directing the potential of this energy toward something positive, from which all parties involved equally benefit. This is why it is helpful when one is influenced by another for the right reasons.

When a wife truly understands her role in the marital relationship, she has great opportunity to influence her husband in the right direction.

Since men are driven to accomplish, they want to win the heart of the apple of their eye, or the fair damsel. They desire to hear her oohs and aahs when they bring home any sort of gift, be it flowers, plants, jewelry, or whatever. They desire to hear her speak of them as if they are the end-all. Most men will do anything, risking life, limb, and reputation or spending whatever, to gain the attention of the one they love.

It is this very drive to win the object of their passion that needs to be kept in check. It is the ability to focus this passion that can help make this happen. When a man starts his journey to win the heart of a woman, the object of his desire, there is nothing stronger than this passion and drive. Again, it is this passion that needs to be focused, but if this passion is allowed to spin out of control, it may become a trap into which both can fall, leading eventually to ruin since it is the love of money that is the root of all evil.

Remember, money in and of itself is not evil, for it is inanimate; therefore, it has no power. It is no different from a rock, a scoop of sand, or a piece of driftwood. Anyone can decide what has value and what does not. Remember the Pet Rock era? If not, Google it. A wise woman can help keep the train on the right track. She can help keep his focus on the family as well as on virtuous values.

With the realization of her role, a wife has great opportunity to influence her husband in the right direction. If her attention is not on material possessions, the accumulation of wealth, or the appearance of affluence, then he might not be as inclined to make her happy in that way.

As wealth grows, men often have a tendency to stray off course, getting caught up in the feeling of power and arrogance, as these are frequently a by-product of wealth. There is a smug confidence they now feel due to having money. Their lives no longer revolve around the family, but around how far they can grow their empire. The focus is on how big he, alone, can become.

The gaining of wealth often causes men to develop the false feeling of power, thus causing them to stray off the right course.

Do not misunderstand me. There are thousands who have accumulated wealth without becoming arrogant or conceited. They are still as humble as ever. They have accomplished all of which they were capable. These people usually give it everything they have until their life on earth is complete. This is the exception, however, not the rule.

The rule is that men by nature can be influenced, but usually only if they had a tendency to go there on their own anyway. What seems to bring this about quicker than anything is the influence of money or sex. History is full of evil women for whom men have killed, conquered empires, or lost their lives, but the wise wife will help direct her husband's passion toward that which is best for the entire family. She will set aside her own personal longings and desires in order to ensure both work together to best provide for their children and their future legacy.

More often than not, men allow this drive for the accumulation of money to get out of control; hence, money is one of their foremost weaknesses. It is the reason men wind up leaving their first love, their wife. She is often the very reason they sought to achieve great accomplishments in the first place. She is the very reason they were in search of more, which at this point only the accumulation of money seems to satiate. Unfortunately, the desire is never satiated for long, and the search continues, while the husband leaves the family behind. Learning to focus this passion and energy is one of the hardest things anyone, male or female, will ever do, but it is also one of the most rewarding.

Those who have become the great artists, musicians, architects, etc., of our world are those who have learned this truth. There are even great artists of today and yesterday, such as Kenny G, Yo-Yo Ma, Beethoven, Chopin, and Vladimir Horowitz, who have found their greatness in focusing all their passion toward the gift they already had. Their lives and the lives of many millions have been enriched by the very fact that they followed their passion.

The bottom line is that money should only be a by-product of the efforts and gifts one applies while serving the world around him. Money alone should not be the only thing sought as a result of one's labor investment. In other words, the reward gained by serving should be a greater reward than the monies paid for what one does. In this manner, money is no longer a weakness, for it has become the tool of disciplined focus. It is much easier to do this when there is a master mind formed by the husband and wife. This gives the united force of two to overcome and focus the passion in the right direction.

Men often allow their drive for money to get out of control, thus the reason money eventually becomes one of their foremost weaknesses.

CHAPTER 15

⟡

Men Have Three Basic Weaknesses: Sex (Part 1)

IF THERE IS ONE thing that men think about, dream about, talk about, seek, desire, or will go to any lengths to get, it is sex. It is also why this is one of man's three basic weaknesses. In his over twenty-five-year search for what makes a man successful, Napoleon Hill found most men do not think with the brain God gave them as much as they are greatly influenced by their drive for sexual gratification or conquest.

In fact, most men reach their midforties prior to controlling the passion behind their sex drive. Until then, their energies are not focused on that which would bring forth a positive result. Their focus is on immediate gratification, which will not invest well in the land of today and, thus, will not bring a harvest for their tomorrows.

> **A highly sexed man may also be a highly successful man
> if he can learn to focus his passion and energies in the
> right direction. The challenge for most men is to learn
> to channel their sexual drive and energy toward serving
> their fellow man. This is at the root of success.**

It is a general rule that most men respond as follows: A man is eating, but as he eats or shortly thereafter, his mind returns to sex. A man is sleeping, but even during sleep his dreams are often of a sexual nature. A man is at work, but his mind often wanders back to sex. A man may be playing golf, but the mind quickly gets back to sex. Whatever the next thing that pops into his head might be, it will only be short-lived, as his mind turns right back to sex.

A man's thoughts can be on anything for a short period, but it isn't long before his thoughts come back around to sex. Such is the makeup of most men. And in the world in which we live today, visual media helps to fuel the intensity.

Unless you are living in a cave, you surely have noticed our media is driven by sex. This obviously exacerbates the man's preoccupation with sex. Sex permeates every aspect of television, from the daily and evening television shows to the made-for-TV movies and advertisements. Even radio ads, billboards, and music are driven by sex. Why is this? Well, sex sells!

One only needs to go to any magazine rack to find the covers of the magazines, regardless of type, plastered with articles about sex. It is amazing how a magazine about running can have an article about sex or a very sensuous picture of a woman on the cover. In a recent visit to Barnes & Noble, I saw a magazine on running that had an article simply called "Running for Better Sex." Even a magazine about food has articles about what type of food one should eat to enjoy the best sex. Car magazines have scantily clad women next to the cars or sitting on or in them. Airplane magazines have pictures of sensuous and erotically dressed female pilots. Sex can be seen in every type and style of magazine, be it overt or covert. Our media experts know sex sells, and it is quite obvious they use it.

Sex is used overtly and covertly to sell anything to anybody, regardless of what is being sold or to whom. Sex is also often used by one spouse to manipulate the other to get what they want.

Most would say sex is used because we are predominantly a male-run society, but nothing could be further from the truth when you consider the amount of magazines and newspapers either owned or run by women. There are also many large advertisement companies owned by women. They all know sex sells, and they use it to sell their magazines and the ads in them.

Now that we have opened the subject on sex being used to sell, it should not be hard to see how anything that has such tremendous power also has the potential to be used for something a little more devious than overt selling.

As shocking as it sounds—and I say this tongue in cheek—women use sex every day on a covert level to manipulate men into doing what they want. This is to say, women often withhold sex in order to get what they desire. This totally distorts the beauty and healthiness of a loving sexual relationship.

> **Using sex as a weapon will destroy all intimacy and may cause severe emotional and psychological problems in one or both.**

Not too long after we were married, my wife and I started attending a class for young married couples at our church. As we all know, there are often some interesting people in any gathering, and this class proved to be no exception. It was from one of those couples that we learned a few things not to do if we were to have a long, happy, and healthy marriage.

After several weeks of hanging out with a certain couple, my wife and I began to share some of the interesting or quirky things we heard them say or do with each other. My wife was hearing things from the female side, while I was hearing things from the male side. I shared how the husband commented to me that his wife was not very sexual and seldom, if ever, wanted to make love. He went so far as to say she was cold and frigid. It was obvious he was not happy. They showed no signs of a warm, loving relationship. It was true each one was nice in their own right, but underneath it all both were wounded. As a result, they were striking out at each other like caged or injured animals.

What my wife was being told was even more interesting. This lady believed she knew how to control her husband and, for that matter, all men. Her methodology was to use sex as a weapon. In their relationship, the beautiful, therapeutic act of making love had been turned into a sexual weapon, if you will. If this isn't the worst thing, then it is close to the worst thing any woman could do in her marriage. It will never work for her benefit, nor is it healthy for the marital union.

> **Making love is turned into sex when it is used as a weapon. The act of making love is true communion between two people who respect and love each other.**

Using sex as a weapon is taking something beautiful that God created and using it for something other than its originally intended use. Sex— or, better stated, the act of making love—was not intended to be used as a weapon, or even as a means of making money, for that matter. It is true communion between two people, especially husband and wife. It is most healing and rejuvenating, not only physically, but emotionally and spiritually, when it is entered into with a healthy respect and love for each other.

> **"Husbands and wives often appear like two broken hearts looking like houses where nobody lives."**
> **—Roger Miller**

On the other hand, when sex is used for the purpose of manipulation, it is overwhelmingly damaging. The damage is not only to the emotional and psychological stability of each person, but it often leads to the destruction of the love and harmony between the couple, which is seldom reparable. Using sex as a tool will always cause a broken relationship. The result will bring eventual divorce, even if this divorce is only in spirit. When two people in such a relationship decide to stay together, the end result is that each person will live separately from the other. They may be under the same roof, but they will not share the same heart. They will be two broken hearts, looking like houses where nobody lives.

Our society uses sex to sell everything. Knowing that this is one of the fundamental weaknesses of men, a wife can be more than instrumental in helping to keep her husband's focus. The wise wife will recognize what she can and should do to help her husband stay on the straight and narrow while dealing with and overcoming his weaknesses. She will see it as her privilege to keep him loved and satisfied, which in the long run will keep him coming home, because the home fires are always burning. Because she keeps the home and herself in good shape, the husband is enticed to always come home.

> **The act of making love should be the culmination of total communication between two people who are in love.**

Following that which is written here will enable both spouses to work like a good team, where one's strength will balance the other's weakness. Showing this kind of attitude toward each other is no different from parents recognizing a weakness in one of their children. What parent wouldn't do their level best to help that child deal with this weakness? Similarly, one spouse is doing the same for the other. It is no different. Surely, there are a few men who are never satisfied, regardless of what their wife may do for them, but the majority will be grateful and appreciative. It is a team effort, and when approached as such, it works well. It is also part of the making of the master mind.

CHAPTER 16

Men Have Three Basic Weaknesses:
Sex (Part 2)

THE ACT OF SEX, the thinking process, as well as the reason for having sex are generally different for a man than for a woman. Sex for a man is usually more of a physiological release, whereas for a woman it is the end of total communication—hence, the romantic needs of her female side. A man doesn't care to talk or romance; he simply cares about getting down to business. Therefore, the stimulus for men is much different than it is for women, for just about anything can spark an erotic interest in a man. Because of this, I believe a great term for men is "eyerotic," or sight stimulated. That is to say it doesn't take much to get their engine running. Women, on the other hand, are "earotic," for they are more stimulated through hearing.

For a man sex is more of a physiological release, while for a woman it is the act of total communication.

In the case of most women, the entire sexual experience starts primarily with what she hears, for what she hears influences what she believes in her head and heart. A woman needs the setup, if you will; she needs the attention. It is important for her to hear certain things as well as feel certain things through the act of gentle touch all during the day or for a period of time prior to "the encounter." In contrast, sound and touch aren't necessary for getting the engine started in a guy, for his heart and ears have very little to do with it, especially in comparison to a woman.

When it comes to sex, not much can keep a man's mind too far from it, regardless of what may happen. It seems men can disassociate themselves from just about anything, easily directing their attention back to sex. I offer an example that happened many years ago on our way home from spending an evening out with friends. We dropped off our friends and were heading home. My mind was focused on getting my wife into bed and getting down to business. The entire drive, though not long, seemed longer than it was due to the anticipation. To make matters tougher, we were about to get caught up in something that would make the drive even longer.

As we were traveling on the interstate, a horrible accident occurred less than thirty seconds in front of us. This accident involved seven cars as well as a gas tanker truck. Eleven people were killed, and many others were critically injured. The flames were so intense and burning so hot that the concrete had to be repaired prior to the reopening of that freeway. Metal from the vehicles melted into puddles, sticking to the concrete and causing it to crack and weaken.

All we remember seeing was a large explosion just ahead and then flames shooting high into the sky. Fortunately, we were over a hundred yards away, and it was late at night so there was very little traffic; therefore, we were able to avoid what could have been as disastrous for us as it was for those directly involved.

The intensity of the heat caused those cars that were closer to burst into flames, instantly engulfing those inside as their cars burned to the ground. The hideous sight of the burning cars, knowing people were in them, and the overwhelming carnage was hard to comprehend. Both of us were shaken to the core. The freeway closed, and all of us were rerouted through side streets.

Just getting those of us who were closer to the wreck off the freeway was a chore. As a result, it took us longer to get home, giving us more time to think about what had just happened. Oddly enough, when we finally arrived home—an hour and forty-five minutes of driving time later, with only four miles of travel—I put the accident out of my mind, returning to that which I had been thinking about previously: making love to my wife.

When it comes to the act of making love, women need romance, while for men, there is no need to waste time on small talk. It is at this juncture that both need to work out their differences.

To say my wife thought I was nuts is an understatement. She was in shock to think I could disassociate myself so easily from what we had just witnessed. She could not get the pictures out of her mind. My friskiness level was at ten, while hers was less than zero. I could not figure out why she was so attached to what happened since it didn't involve either one of us or anyone we knew.

Fortunately, we sat down and discussed the differences of how each felt and the reasons our thoughts might be what they were. We recognized men's thoughts and inclinations were different from women's. In the end, she felt it would be better to make love, but I was not sure if, in fact, this was the right thing to do. Together, we prayed about the situation, and we allowed some time to elapse before ultimately deciding to make love.

Some wives are gracious enough to satisfy their husband's sexual desires even though they may not be feeling up to par, are very tired, or are simply not in the mood. In some cases, the husband may never know how his wife is really feeling, especially if she falls into his arms, fully submitting to his advances, and loving freely, without reservation or hesitation. On the other hand, a husband should not take advantage of the goodness of his wife. If the wife is willing to give this much of herself, then the husband should be doing the same. It takes 110 percent from each to make the relationship work. The husband should be learning more about her every day, becoming sensitive to her wants and needs and responding accordingly.

This is no different from what we all do at work. We often go to work not feeling up to par, or we just may not feel like working, but we do our job anyway. Interestingly enough, neither the husband nor the wife apply this same discipline in their marriage. If they did, giving it their best, just think of the positive results we would see and the marriages that would be saved. By not giving it their best, however, they wind up in a relationship that fails in the same manner their employment would fail. With such an attitude on the job, their performance would suffer and their position would eventually be filled by someone else.

**The marital relationship requires the same commitment
and discipline that you give to your job if the marriage is
to be successful.**

This is exactly what happens in the marriage where little effort is applied. As unfortunate as it is, someone is always standing by to take our place when we are not doing what we should be doing with regard to our relationship and the one to whom we once committed our love.

Once again, I can see the wheels spinning as well as hear the remarks of many women who do not feel it should be their job to make sure their husband is happy. I can also hear the remarks of the husbands who are thinking the same. Nothing, however, could be further from the truth. If you are employed, you are making your employer happy. If you are not making your employer happy, you will be replaced. It does not get any simpler. A happy employer makes for a happy job. A happy spouse makes for a happy home.

It is our job to work at being our best for our spouse, in the same manner we are for our employer. Unfortunately, we usually give our best to our employers and others, while giving the least to our spouse and family. In many instances, these types of relationships wind up platonic, with both doing their own thing and living their own lives yet inhabiting the same home.

Looking at this from another direction, what about those who volunteer? They give freely of themselves yet expect nothing in return, and they do this even when they don't feel like it. Can we not do the same in our relationships, especially our marriage? Of course we can, and we should.

Unfortunately, most do not do this even for those they love, simply because past experience has proven they will get nothing in return. If, however, you look at this the way those who are volunteering do, you will find they are not doing this for any other reason than the personal satisfaction of giving. Can our marital interaction be the same? Why is it we do not give simply for the satisfaction of giving? Why do we not look at it as giving to bless someone else the way we do when we volunteer? By doing so, we would be bringing a blessing into our own lives, in turn.

Further, if you are aware of the seed-sowing principle, then you already know that when you plant, you always get it back in one way or another. It is important to remember that the giving must be with the right attitude, for this keeps the seed watered and cultivated. When we give, although it may not come back from the one to whom we gave, it will come back, for such is the sowing and reaping principle.

We should now be able to see that a marriage requires just as much effort as our job. It should be of no surprise to find our marriage suffering while our job survives, based on what we give to work versus what we give to our marriage.

If you do not give to your marital relationship with the same passion you give to others, then what else could you expect than to be potentially replaced by someone who will do a better job?

Although the act of sex, the thinking process, and the reasons for having sex are often different for the male versus the female, when both work at understanding these differences and find common ground on which to build their relationship, they can grow together and individually.

CHAPTER 17

Men Have Three Basic Weaknesses: Ego

MAN'S THIRD BASIC WEAKNESS is ego. Ego is essential to the makeup of a man's nature and character; therefore, it is easy to conclude that every man needs an ego. Without a healthy level of ego, men would be like puppets with no master, marionettes with no strings. Unfortunately, most men have a tendency to think they are much more than they are due to an overabundance of ego. Often, this is a man's way of overcompensating for what may be lacking in other areas of his life. For instance, he may have a poor self-image, and his way of dealing with it is to portray himself to be something he is not.

> **Ego is essential to the makeup of a man's nature and character. Without a healthy ego, men are as puppets with no master or marionettes with no strings.**

Before we go any further, it is essential that we take a look at the meaning of "ego":

1. It is the self, especially as distinct from the world and other selves.
2. In psychoanalysis, it is the division of the psyche that is conscious and most immediately controls thought and behavior; it is the part that is most in touch with external reality.
3. It is an exaggerated sense of self-importance or conceit.
4. It is an appropriate pride in oneself with a healthy self-esteem.

It is the third definition that most people associate with ego, and it is this type of ego with which most men struggle. No one, male or female, should have an issue with the "self" being distinct from the rest of the world. Like snowflakes, we are all unique. On the other hand, when it comes to ego, very few would even know of the psychoanalytic aspect. It is the fourth definition, however, that we need to know. Everyone needs healthy self-esteem, as well as a sense of pride, but these need to be at an appropriate level. The appropriate level allows one to be unique, distinct from others, in the same manner as each snowflake differs, but nonetheless they are still snowflakes. People should feel comfortable being around you (as opposed to an inflated ego that causes separation), due to the fact others feel uncomfortable around you.

Because of ego and pride, men have often walked away from the best thing that ever happened to them: the woman of their dreams. It is also because of ego and pride that men will not say they're sorry. Travis Tritt, the country singer, said it quite clearly in his song titled "Foolish Pride": "Chalk another love lost up to foolish pride." Due to having an inflated ego, men will pick fights, take dares, or in general do wild, crazy, or just plain foolish things. In most cases, these childish tantrums often lead to a life of misery, sorrow, imprisonment, or even death.

The misery and sorrow are often caused by the fact that they are too stubborn to say the word "sorry." They play the tough-guy role and wind up losing the girl of their dreams, all because their ego-inflamed temper caused them to do something stupid and they wound up in jail or prison. It is the wrong type of ego that causes many to bite off more than they should, for this type of ego makes them too proud to back down. It is this same type of ego that causes one to drive when he is drunk. Unfortunately, by doing so, men wind up paying the ultimate price through the death of others, loved ones, or self.

> **Having a healthy ego is seldom the issue, as most men wind up with a bigger ego than their level of knowledge, skill, talent, or ability; thus, they wind up using their ego to make up for their shortcomings.**

Ego, like most things, has its bad and good sides. We all know there is such a thing as too much of anything. Paul the Apostle said nothing in and of itself is bad, but when anything is taken to the extreme, it can be. Thus, when we allow anything to control us, especially this type of ego, we lose.

Allow me to give you a few examples of things that can be bad and good. Let us first take a look at ordinary tires, like the ones on your car. The correct air pressure in a tire is just as important as the correct level of ego. Filling the tire above that for which it is rated is not good, as it not only reduces the amount of tire on the road, it wears the tire in the center, thus causing the tire to lose traction in wet conditions. To make matters worse, filling the tire with too much air could cause the tire to explode, not only destroying the tire but hurting or killing those around.

On the other hand, not enough air in the tire can be just as bad, for this causes excessive wear on the outside and can cause the sidewall structure of the tire to break down. Both conditions result in uneven wear and can lead to very dangerous driving situations.

Another example is the hot air balloon. It takes hot air—and a lot of it—to cause the balloon to rise. The issue here is too much hot air can cause the balloon to rise too high and get caught in winds and jet streams, which can take the balloon far off course or above one's ability to receive enough oxygen. The result of this type of uncontrolled hot air filling can be death or severe injury, just like an overinflated ego.

In contrast, if the balloon does not get enough hot air, it will never lift off the ground. The hot air balloon without enough hot air is similar to a man without an ego—he will have no drive or initiative to do anything. In short, the person with a poor self-image or no self-esteem is devoid of a true ego. This is a person short of having what it takes to lift him from the doldrums of life to any level of success.

The person having a poor self-image or no self-esteem is a person devoid of a true and honest ego.

Before we discuss how women can properly handle a man's ego, we need to discuss the four types of women a man might encounter. They are Ms. Dominator, Ms. Passive, Ms. Enabler, and Ms. Exhorter.

CHAPTER 18

---◇◈◇---

Four Types of Women

THERE ARE FOUR TYPES of women who, because of their personality, have four distinct effects on their husband's ego. These four types are Ms. Dominator, Ms. Passive, Ms. Enabler, and Ms. Exhorter. I shall describe these women, what it is they do, as well as the effects they have on their husbands.

The personality of the wife will always have a distinct effect on the husband's behavior for bad or good.

Ms. Dominator

This type of woman dominates and bullies her husband. If a man happens to be married to Ms. Dominator, he is living with a woman who belittles him and puts him down every time he tries to do better. She does her best to shred his ego, leaving him with little motivation. In order to avoid this treatment, he becomes silent, for she has beaten down his spirit. She takes a machete to his ego daily, which in turn deflates his passion for growing, as well as his motivation to conquer and overcome. Since opposites attract, it is possible the man attracted this strong and overbearing woman.

From the beginning he does not take the lead in the relationship. As time passes it becomes obvious he is a leadership failure, as he has neglected to take the responsibility of a leadership role. In order to keep things moving forward and provide some strength and direction, Ms. Dominator gladly accepts the position. Unfortunately, because she has had to take over the leadership, she begins to lose respect for him, and she winds up cutting him down even more as each day goes by.

The dominated husband is usually harsh or curt toward women at work or in other places outside his home, for he believes this gives him back some of his ego.

Sadly, he does nothing, since he is not the type to argue. He does, however, take it out on many of the women with whom he works or others he meets to make himself feel better, in hopes of gaining back some level of ego. This is usually very evident in the place where he works.

Ms. Passive

This woman becomes a doormat and is run over by the man as he takes all of the land she allows him to take. In other words, she accepts all of his verbal abuse. In the case of exceptionally passive women, men often push just to see how far their wife will let them go. They often take and take until they are bored with taking. As they take more and more of their wife's dignity, their own ego grows.

Unfortunately, the husband in these cases usually places no boundaries on himself. He is often the one to run around, since he does not respect his wife. Interestingly, I believe God put these types together, because she needed his input and he needed hers, but he did not respond to her by building her up and she did not stand her ground. They both wind up being each other's worst enemy instead of each other's helpmate.

Ms. Enabler

This type of person enables, allows, permits, and empowers the weak and undisciplined husband to abuse alcohol, drugs, or both. It is quite common during these times of abuse for him to physically or verbally abuse her. More often than not, these men run around on their wives, as well. It makes them feel like more than they are. When he is sober and the wife finally confronts him, he cries and swears he will never do it again, but alas he always does, and she always takes him back.

It is usually at this point Ms. Enabler finds herself in a prison of her own making by allowing him to use her as his punching bag. She could have put a stop to his growing ego early on; she could have said this kind of behavior and treatment is unacceptable, but she did not. Now, after many years, and having traveled way down the road, it seems it is too late. Sadly, she becomes a large part of the problem rather than contributing to the solution. This, however, does not excuse the man for being a lowlife.

Ms. Exhorter

This type of wife can be of enormous help to her husband in many ways in that she will appeal to his better senses, provide admonishment, and give excellent advice when necessary. Being an exhorter is a great gift, as it allows the wife to help her husband keep his ego in check in the proper manner. As previously stated, a man needs an ego, but not one the size of Texas. There is a need for humility, and an overinflated ego keeps one from being humble.

The wise wife recognizes her husband needs an ego, but one that is of a manageable size. She helps him to keep it in check by using simple requests placed at the most opportune times. For example, some years ago I spoke at the McCormack Center in Chicago to architects, engineers, building owners and managers, as well as contractors. There were over five thousand in attendance. The presentation was well received, as I received a standing ovation at the end of the presentation. I also answered questions for nearly two hours afterward.

To say I was pumped would be an understatement. I felt incredible. I was superhuman, at least in my own mind. I had worked on this presentation incessantly for fourteen months, and it was well received by all who attended. My head was huge; I couldn't wait to get home.

When my wife picked me up at the airport, I began to tell her about how the presentation garnered me a standing ovation. My wife listened to how incredible I was all the way home. She realized there was going to be a problem getting my head in the door, so she waited until we arrived home to say, "I am so proud of you. I know how hard you have worked and for how long. I also know you are a good speaker. Anyone would want to hear you. I am so happy for you."

She left her comments of how good I was there and moved on to that which brought me back to reality. "Oh, by the way, sweetheart, before you come in the house, could you get the trash cans out of the garage and put them out front so they can be picked up? I also need you to get some things out of the trunk of my car and bring them in the house when you bring in your luggage. I will keep the door open to make it easier. Thank you, honey."

> **The exhorter wife knows when *and* how to check the tire pressure to see how much air there is above the recommended levels. She is good at letting out just enough air to get hubby back to the normal level, but does not use a punch or knife to deflate the tire.**

Notice, in order to get me back to reality and out of my inflated perception of myself, she didn't cut me down by verbally belittling me or telling me I was worthless. She was wise in her choice of words, bringing me down to earth by letting me know I was still her husband, still the father of our two little girls, and still had responsibilities at home, which did not go away because some people a few thousand miles away were impressed.

When she first started asking me to take out the trash, I felt a pang of disappointment, but then it dawned on me what she had done. She had helped me reduce my ego just enough to enter the house and join the family. Although my ego was reduced, it was barely enough to get my head in the door.

The next day she handed me a honey-do list. She said she had made it weeks ago, but I think she either got up early or stayed up late and wrote down some things to help me come back to reality. This is how to keep a man's ego in check. Check the tire pressure by listening. Then, when you see how much there is above the recommendation, let a little out, but don't take a knife and stab the tire. Your husband needs air in his ego to get around and carry on his life. This is correct spousal interaction at its finest. I am grateful to be able to say I married that woman.

> **The exhorted husband is often quite successful, having a balanced ego, which allows him to properly interact with the rest of the world.**

CHAPTER 19

⸺⸱❖⸱⸺

The Desire to Change Him

WE HAVE SPOKEN ABOUT men and their three biggest weaknesses, but what about the women? Well, rather than discuss weaknesses, let's discuss what character traits women could seek that would be helpful in building up both their own self-esteem and the relationship. It just so happens there are a few to which a wife can aspire. One of the most important is allowing her husband to be the person he is and not someone she wants to change him into or hopes he will become.

In order to understand why a woman would want to change her husband, you need to know something about the female thought process. With a little understanding you will see why most want their husbands to be someone else.

Renowned author and relationship and marriage counselor Dr. Gary Smalley explains in his book If Only He Knew the four greatest needs of women:

1. Emotional and physical security
2. Regular and meaningful communication
3. Nonsexual touch
4. Romance

When you think of this in light of what we have just said about men, you can see why there are issues and differences in the thought process. For most women, this starts when she is first attracted to the guy. She likes what she sees, but after some observation she realizes he needs a little of this and a little of that—in essence, a little nip here in his demeanor and a few little tucks in his attitude and sophistication. Her thought is

76

she will win him over and he will change, because she will have enough of a hold on him to make him do so.

It is as if women have a mental image of what their ideal husband should be and will work to bring about the necessary changes in his life to make her mental image of him become reality.

> **One of the best things a wife can do (but has a tough time with) is allowing her husband to be himself without trying to change him into the perfect man she has pictured. After all, she was attracted to whom he was, not what she wants him to be.**

I would venture to say there are many of us who know a woman who has married a not-so-desirable man, a man whom she loved even though he treated her with disrespect. In every case the woman believed she could change him, but alas it does not happen. Men by nature do not change. A man might act as if he is going to, he may say he is going to, but he does not and will not. He may even go underground with what he is doing, thereby making the marriage lonelier and emptier. He will act one way around her and another way around his friends. In other words, he still does what he was doing, but he simply does it when she is not around. After all, she wasn't supposed to be his best friend—at least that is his thinking. She winds up with a broken heart, feeling like she lives alone or in, as Roger Miller put it, "a house where nobody lives."

The way most women work on getting a man to change is by nagging. Think of it. How does your conscience work? It works by gnawing and nagging at you until you either do something about it or you harden your heart enough so as not to hear it anymore. Hardening your heart or suppressing the conscience is what happens when a woman nags. It is exactly the same.

> **Men, by nature, do not change, yet women will do what they can to bring about change even at the cost of her life.**

The woman's thought process is, If I nag enough, he will change. I hate to repeat myself, but the only change that is going to come is that the husband will continue to do what he has been doing, with one exception: it will not be around his wife. When he is around his wife, he will do what she wants. He will act as if he is listening when he is not. This is similar to the way a mother learns to listen to her children. She listens just enough. Her ears have been trained to respond based on real need, not whining.

I have been most fortunate in that my wife has never been one to nag. She has been one to state her case and leave it. This is the best way to get a positive response from the husband. When a wife takes the nagging route or goes toe-to-toe with her husband in debate, it seldom brings about the expected results. As a matter of fact, it can cause the little inward demon in any person (the husband in this case) to rise up as he goes into defense mode, getting louder and louder, standing bolder and stronger in order to win. After all, he is the man, and in his eyes he should win. It is as if she has backed a tiger into a corner with no way out, so he screams and argues.

This begs the question, "What if her nagging is what I need to affect a change in me?" That is a great question, which warrants a legitimate answer. We need what we get from each other in order to help us to grow, but men will not change because a wife decides to nag him. A man must make the decision to change on his own, not because of his wife's nagging.

If, however, the wife is wise enough to affect a change by stating her case and holding her ground without nagging, then the idea will often sink into his subconscious mind. Eventually he will wind up changing, believing the change came of his own volition. The truth is, if a man succumbs and changes because of the nagging, he relinquishes his masculine side and subordinates to the feminine side. As a general rule, this is not going to happen. David Deida speaks quite strongly of this in his book Dear Lover.

> **The truth is, a man must change on his own terms and from within. If he does not, those following him will lose their trust and belief in his leadership ability. This goes for the wife, as well.**

If the man does give in and change, the woman eventually loses respect for him and his leadership. The marriage suffers and crumbles unless the husband makes an about-face and steps up to the plate again.

It is true men need to grow, but they should do so through their own study and desire, along with the help of their wife, family, and friends. The growth should not be the result of pressure, nagging, or preaching from the wife or anyone else. The man is supposed to leave his mother and father and cleave unto his wife, not allow her to be his mom. He can learn from her, but she shouldn't be raising him to be what she thinks he is supposed to be. He is not her son or child to raise.

Interestingly enough, the person the wife usually wants hubby to become is not the person to whom she was originally attracted. The fact that opposites attract is the reason there are issues, and these differences, when properly responded to, help us to grow.

CHAPTER 20

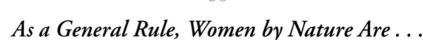

As a General Rule, Women by Nature Are . . .

IN THIS CHAPTER AND the next we will discuss the general rules that govern most women and men. There are exceptions to every rule, but generally women and men follow these patterns.

As a general rule, women by nature are the following:

Joiners. Being right-brained, women like to feel connected, which is why they join groups, to be around people. Women love to talk or just hang out, always wanting to belong or be part of something. They are usually the ones wanting to go to church, attend a play, or hang out with friends, while hubby wants to stay home to watch sports or go to the driving range to hit golf balls.

Not conservative. More often than not, women are the ones to spend money when it is not there. They are also not conservative in thought, meaning they are quick to rationalize away reality or facts. They are not ones to think things all the way through to their logical conclusion.

Liberal. Women are the quickest to give a little rather than hold the line. When it comes to most women, there is no such thing as black and white, but there is a whole lot of room for gray—that is to say, room for change or compromise.

Guilt-prone. The fact that women, by nature, are guilt-prone is the very reason attorneys like to load up juries with women. Women have a tendency to feel sorry for defendants if they do a good job of acting. As a matter of fact, the toughest part of the defense attorney's job is getting his client to put on a tear-jerking performance so the female jurors will feel sorry for him.

Romantic. They are stimulated by conversation, not necessarily by sight, unless it was a path of rose petals leading to a table set with white linen and candles. It is predominantly what a woman hears that will stir her passions—hence, the desire to see a romantic movie, not one of violence, sex, or oppression. Women are "earotic." They get aroused through what they hear, not necessarily what they see. They can be stimulated by what they read, but it is what they hear that really gets their engines humming. A wise man would do well to learn that a woman's ears are the most effective organ for sexual stimulation.

Talkers. Women are usually the most talkative in the marriage. I have a friend who says his wife talks all the time, especially when they drive. On the other hand, she says he will sit in the driver's seat on a three-hour drive without saying a word to her as she talks the entire three hours. His response to her talking while he is driving is always the same: "If I only had a gun or a ball-peen hammer, just a quick ping on the temple and the drive would be much more peaceful." Many women talk so much it is hard to get a word in edgewise, and they don't even know it. Some men do, as well, but that's the exception.

Emotional. We said this before, but there was a time when airlines primarily used women as flight attendants. They were trained to be calm, cool, collected, and ready to handle any adverse situation without losing it, which is not the nature of most women. Since women are emotional, they would overreact to turbulence, quick changes in altitude, changes in pressure, a quick descent, etc. Even though the captain tells the passengers all is fine, the eyes of the passengers would be on the female flight attendants. If they were calm, the passengers would be too.

Here is an example of how this works. You are driving down the road, and all of a sudden your wife blurts out, "Oh my God!" In that instant your heart leaps into your throat, cutting off your ability to breathe, as well as drastically affecting blood flow to the rest of your body. Meanwhile, your head starts spinning and your thoughts are racing as you try to figure out who, what, when, where, and how bad. In a split second your mind has had a thousand thoughts, none of which are good. When you are finally able to catch your breath and push your heart back into your chest, you ask her what is wrong. She says, "Oh, I almost forgot, tomorrow is my mom's birthday." You start looking for the ball-peen hammer.

This is proof positive that women overreact to most things. It is also proof that they are emotional. Everything is a major issue, so if the plane is going down you can bet she will be the first to let you know. The fact that the female flight attendant is cool and calm helps to keep the passengers cool and calm, as well.

Finally, women are not ones to say what they mean or mean what they say. Women say what they feel. Their words are an expression of what they are feeling at the moment they are speaking. For example, she may be expressing how she feels about the marriage, the children, her parents, something at work, or whatever. Women express what they are feeling about things in general, and they do not necessarily answer the specific question the men just asked.

So, now that you know this, don't be harsh or quick to judge. The two of you will be much better off when you understand what is happening and why. She is simply talking even though she may not be making sense or even be on the same subject.

Adding confusion to a woman speaking out of emotion instead of logic is the fact that we do not often truly hear that which is being said. Most of us are not nearly as good at communicating as we think we are, and the reason boils down to the following: what we actually said versus what they actually heard, what we think we said versus what they think they heard, and what they think we said versus what we think they heard.

When you add uncontrolled emotion to the above, it becomes obvious why that which is said is often misconstrued.

If we take the time to think before we speak, and if we take the time to look at the situation from the other's viewpoint, we will better understand how to deal with each other and, more importantly, how to correctly respond to each other. That is the key to a successful marriage.

CHAPTER 21

·◇◈◇·

As a General Rule, Men by Nature Are . . .

WOMEN, BY NATURE, HAVE certain traits, and men do, as well. As a general rule, men are the following:

Loners. There are times when men would rather be alone, even when others are around. I know, for I am often like this. This is not to say men don't like being around people, but those content with who they are do not necessarily have to be around others in order to feel fulfilled or validated. It is why you will frequently hear, "He seems like he is in another world." Men truly can be in another world—their own world. As James Brown so aptly sung it, "this is a man's world." But there is one thing to remember, as well, because it also says men are nothing without a woman.

Since the beginning of recorded history, it has been about the man. Even in the Bible, there is little written about women in comparison to what is written about men. I believe there is a reason for this, and it is not because women are not equal. Rather, the responsibility has always been on the man to lead and direct. Apparently, God found it necessary to tell men what to do, but he did not find it necessary to tell women. Women, it seems, are either already doing it or are ready to do it.

Based on the Bible, it seems God saw it essential to tell men what they needed to do, whereas it doesn't seem God needed to do this to women, for they are either already doing what is necessary or are ready to do it.

In contrast, I know many men who can't stand to be alone for any length of time, even with their spouses. They need others around

83

to validate them. Validation might come from others laughing at their jokes or others verbally interacting with them while they talk up their achievements. It is most unfortunate when men are not able to spend quality alone time (more than one hour) with their spouses. This shows they need to grow to accept whom they are while leaving behind their insecurities. Doing so will have a very positive effect on the marriage and on them personally, as well.

Logical. Men are predominantly left-brained, and therefore they have a tendency to think things all the way through to their logical conclusion. Thinking things through is what helps them to keep things in perspective. It is what helps them to see the potential for danger or pitfalls ahead. It is true in many cases they are not as spiritual or spiritually sensitive as women. They do not seem to have that sixth sense like most women. Being logical, they tend not to exercise faith or believe in that which they cannot see. In that same vein, they are not easily sold a bill of goods, as they are not likely to listen to the sob story or the sales pitch, like most women.

Conservative. Men are not usually the ones spending money simply because the money is there. Men are less likely to be as vain as women. They are not as likely to care about what others might think of them. We are now being bombarded by ads urging men to enter into a metrosexual world, causing more men to become vain about their looks. This isn't true across the board but is made to seem so. Men are conservative by nature, because they are left-brained by nature. This is not to say women are not conservative, but once again we are speaking of the rule and not the exception.

Not prone to guilt. As a general rule, men do not carry around a conscience full of guilt. The greatest example of this was David, the youngest son of Jesse, the small redheaded sheepherder. He was the nearly overlooked reject who went on to become the king of Israel and was later called a man after God's own heart. David had as much blood on his hands as any man previous. He was guilty of such things as adultery, murder, lying, deceit, and fornication, and he was a poor father on top of it all. Yet, he believed that God would forgive and forget what he had done. More importantly, he was able to move forward in his life without allowing his past failures to keep him bound to yesterday. He was able to move into his tomorrows with renewed life and exuberance. This made him a man after God's own heart.

David believed in God's mercy, grace, and suffering long before Christ died on the Cross. Although David lived in the eye-for-an-eye and tooth-for-a-tooth era, he appropriated forgiveness in his own life and toward others in a most remarkable way. His ability to forgive himself allowed him to get on with his life after making huge mistakes. Unfortunately, the vast majority of those who have committed such acts carry the guilt their entire lives, allowing this guilt to choke their ability to have a productive life. This is especially true of women. Carrying the guilt causes ulcers, cancer, and other disorders that negatively affect their abilities and health. They might even run away and hide in a cave in the same manner as David.

The difference between David and most others is that he was eventually able to leave the cave. Rather than hiding in it due to his previous behavior, as many of us have done, he made a decision to get rid of the guilt and get out of the cave. He was able to get out because he openly talked with God about what he had done, acknowledging his shortcomings and accepting God's forgiveness. However, just as important was his ability to forgive himself. Once he did, he did not look back. Rather, he got on with his life.

Now, having said men are not necessarily guilt-prone, it is important to point out that they are prone to dumping guilt. The reason they don't carry guilt is that, more often than not, they are dumping it on someone else. This is usually their wife, their children, or others around them who accept it. If a man is not married, he will dump this on his female friends or weaker male friends who have more of a feminine nature. We see this trait all the way back to Adam, who, when confronted by God, did not accept the guilt of his own sin but blamed it, not only on Eve, but on God. Adam did this in his conversation with God, when he said, "It was the woman you gave me" (Genesis 3:12).

As leaders, directors, and friends, men must take their issues to God and not dump them on others. This is the correct spousal interaction, not dumping a bad day on someone else. Your bad day is what you need to deal with. It isn't someone else's responsibility to deal with it, as most have their own issues. The bottom line is that true leaders do not dump their personal issues and struggles on others.

Quick to anger. I have seen this in the majority of men. Most men are insecure. This is the reason they get angry or loud when challenged by their wife or others. It is the reason they get angry if they feel threatened.

For those who are insecure, this is part of their defense mechanism. The next time you see this in someone, remind yourself they are more than likely insecure and it is their way of dealing with the situation. This doesn't make it right, but it helps you understand why.

Once you see what you are and where you should be, you can seek to become that person necessary to ensure a great marriage. More importantly, you can use it to ensure your own personal growth. For personal growth, you treat others with respect as you learn to feel good about and respect yourself.

Lastly, what is obvious here is the need to grow, to learn to respond in kindness, through the correct spousal interaction. This will keep the fire of the heart burning, the emotions stable, and they will feel fulfilled and secure. By following the path laid out in this book, both husband and wife will not wind up brokenhearted and looking like houses where nobody lives.

Life is too short to live like this. Life is too precious to throw away in such a manner. Make a decision to live life to the fullest while enjoying it with someone you love.

BIBLIOGRAPHY AND
SUGGESTED READING

Branden, Nathaniel, and E. Devers Branden. The Romantic Love Question & Answer Book. J.P. Tarcher Inc., 1982.

Branden, Nathaniel. The Psychology of Romantic Love. Bantam, 1980.

Clifton, Donald O., and Paula Nelson. Soar with Your Strengths. Delacorte Press. 1992.

Corn, Laura. 237 Intimate Questions Every Woman Should Ask a Man. Park Avenue Publishers. January 1, 2000

Deida, David. Blue Truth. Sounds True, 2005.

Deida, David. Dear Lover. Sounds True, 2005.

Dobson, James. What Wives Wish Their Husbands Knew About Women. Tyndale, 1975.

Dweck, Carol. Mindset. Random House, 2006.

Gollwitzer, Helmut. Song of Love: A Biblical Understanding of Sex. Fortress Press, 1979.

Harley, Willard F., Jr. His Needs, Her Needs. Revell Publishers, 1986.

Harley, Willard F., Jr. Love Busters. Revell Publishers, 1992.

Hicks, Roy H. Healing Your Insecurities. Harrison House, 1982.

Hocking, David, and Carole Hocking. Romantic Lovers. Harvest House, 1986.

The Holy Bible.

LaHaye, Beverly. The Spirit-Controlled Woman. Harvest House, 1976.

Landorf, Joyce. Tough & Tender. Revell Publishers, 1975.

Myss, Carolyne. Anatomy of the Spirit. Three Rivers Press, 1996.

Millman, Dan. Way of the Peaceful Warrior. H.J. Kramer, 1980.

Peck, M. Scott. The Road Less Traveled. Simon & Schuster, 1978.

Roberts, Frances J. Come Away My Beloved. Spire Books, 1970.

Schwartz, Pepper. Prime. HarperCollins Publishers, 2007.

Sterling, A. Justin. What Really Works with Men. Warner Books, 1992.

Swindoll, Charles R. Growing Wise in Family Life. Insight for Living, 1973.

Wheat, Ed, and Gaye Wheat. Intended for Pleasure. Revell Publishers, 1977.

Ziglar, Zig. Confessions of a Happy Christian. Bantam Books, 1978.

ABOUT THE AUTHOR

RICK HAS DONE MANY things in his life, from founding and owning companies to pastoring a church for over five years. He was on the radio for seven years, and he made TV appearances on the TBN channel. He has continued to do public speaking at marriage seminars, motivational speaking, and keynote speaking. He has served on the board of several churches as an elder since his late twenties.

From the age of twenty-three, he has taken a personal interest in helping people, especially in their marriage. In his twenties he started counseling couples regarding marriage issues, doing so with those his own age and with many over twice his age.

He has always exhibited keen insight into relationships of all kinds, not just marriages. His ability to recognize and sense the truth behind the issues of those who have come to him for guidance or counseling over these past almost-forty years has been the motivation for the writing of this book.

Rick still counsels and works with couples today regarding issues they are facing in their marriage. When asked to officiate a wedding ceremony, he requires several counseling sessions to ensure the couple will enter into this union with a full understanding of what they are entering into and what it will require of each one personally.